THE KETOGENIC MEDITERRANEAN DIET

Complete Delicious and Easy Recipes to Lead to Healthier Lifestyle

Table of Content

Introduction

Welcome, my lovely reader, to this brief, sweet, and incredibly useful book that should, could, and probably will bring you all the answers you need to improve your keto journey to a healthier Mediterranean lifestyle.

I'm sure that by now, you've become quite frustrated with the fact that no matter what you try, you can't seem to find the perfect eating regiment where you no longer feel guilty about the food that you consume. You've probably attempted different diets and bought into the idea that you would be able find a suitable diet for the heart in the process, only to find to your immediate dismay, that you have not made any progress whatsoever. As a result, you keep procrastinating on it because you are unsure as to whether you have what it takes to stick to such a heavy commitment. The fact of the matter is, you definitely need to stop saying these things to yourself because, contrary to what you might believe, you do have what it takes. Instead of constantly beating yourself up and thinking that you can't do anything to change for the better, why not give this book a go and enrich yourself on how to integrate the Keto Diet with the Mediterranean Diet to get the most use of them into your life so that you can gain the results that you desperately want?

If your desire is to achieve the above, then please keep on reading! You will find your wanted answers! This book combines Mediterranean Diet with Ketogenic Diet, which will tell you all essentials about them, and you will know what the difference and similarity they have and how can they be combined. In the book, you will know many tips and tricks about how to follow this diet, what foods to eat or avoid and some tips for eating out. This book will 100% lead you to a heart hearty goal, to prevent disease and have a healthy living!

Even though you might have already followed a Ketogenic Diet or a Mediterranean Diet before, you may know that most of the foods they allow followers to eat are in low carb high fat food. This is the most important reason why these 2 diets could be combined. This cookbook provides readers with many mouth-watering but easy-to-prepare recipes, which all are in detailed and show you step-by-step procedure. With these dishes, your diet journey will be succeeding easily!

All the recipes in this book are clear and easy to follow. The title is descriptive and indicates the main products used in a dish. Also, there information on how many servings you can expect out of the recipe and gives the approximate preparation time and cooking time. The List of Ingredients is made by the order of use of each item and the preparation method are given by the order of the individual steps. All the recipes can be divided easily or multiplied, and the great majority of them freeze well.

If you really want an effective and actionable solution to change to a totally healthy living, then you should consider this Heart Healthy Mediterranean Ketogenic diet program, which will really change your whole life overwhelmingly! Let's get started now! Wish you a pleasant diet journey!

Fundamentals of the Diets

The Mediterranean diet

The Mediterranean diet is one of the healthiest dietary patterns inspired by traditional healthy eating practices. The Mediterranean cooking methods were developed by residents of countries bordering the Mediterranean Sea, such as France, Italy, Greece, Spain, Turkey, Egypt, and Lebanon. The Mediterranean diet allows you to consume a wide variety of nutritionally balanced foods. It is one of the most economical diets that allow you to consume seasonable plant-based foods like fresh fruits, vegetables, nuts, beans, whole grains, whole foods, fish, olive oil, etc. The diet also allows moderate consumption of protein and low consumption of dairy products.

Highly processed foods, artificial sweeteners, and processed meat are restricted in the Mediterranean diet. Mediterranean foods are good sources of essential vitamins, fibers, minerals, and nutrients and have antioxidant properties. The diet allows a limited red meat intake and moderate fish consumption in olive oil. It is better to consume fish because of its omega-3 fatty acids. This is good for heart health and reduces the risk of a heart attack. Preventing type-2 diabetes and also reducing the risk of cancer. The Mediterranean diet focuses on the consumption of whole foods and healthy fats, which aid in weight loss.

Historically the Mediterranean diet is one of the most ancient dietary patterns and eating habits of the people living in the Mediterranean Sea. It is located between Asia, Africa, and the European continent. The Mediterranean diet's origins may be traced back to ancient civilizations such as the Romans, Greeks, Egyptians, and others. Some historical records from ancient Roman and Greek philosophers stress the importance of the Mediterranean diet, which is rich in seasonal fresh foods and has a variety of health benefits. There is an influence of Moorish and Arab culture in the Mediterranean region. The Moorish and Arab cultures introduced new ingredients, such as citrus fruits, rice, almonds, and spices like saffron, cumin, and cinnamon, to the Mediterranean diet.

The Mediterranean region is popular for its ideal climate and soil conditions suitable for olive cultivation. Nearly 90 percent of the world's olives are produced in Mediterranean nations like Greece, Italy, Spain, Tunisia, and Turkey. Due to their mild climate conditions, seasonable fruits and vegetables are available during all four seasons. All these regions are at the banks of the Mediterranean Sea, so fish is one of the components of the Mediterranean diet. Fishing is one of the occupations in which most people live in these areas.

The Mediterranean diet encompasses more than just the foods consumed. It recognizes the importance of enjoying meals with friends and family and encourages a sense of community. The social aspect of the Mediterranean diet adds to its overall enjoyment and establishes a positive relationship with food. The Mediterranean diet has garnered significant attention and recognition from medical professionals and researchers due to its numerous health benefits.

Makes up of Mediterranean Diet?

Unsaturated fats from olive oil and omega-3 fatty acids from fish are two key dietary ingredients in the Mediterranean diet; sunshine and vitamin D are two key ingredients for the Mediterranean lifestyle. Medical research is still on into finding why unsaturated fats and omega-3 fatty acids are healthy for the heart but it appears the two lower the amount of bad cholesterol, LDL, and protect arteries from inflammation that leads to atherosclerosis. Heart disease is extremely complex but the root cause seems to be an unbalanced diet poor in healthy fats, such as that gotten from vegetables and fish. Sunshine stimulates circulation and lifts up the mood while vitamin D serves as a protection for the heart and the immune system. These four things—unsaturated fats, omega-3 fatty acids, sunshine, and vitamin D—appear to be the healthiest combo for longevity, fitness, and good mood.

The Ketogenic Diet

The ketogenic diet exploits the process of ketosis to help people lose weight or manage specific medical issues. It is a high-fat, low-carb, moderate-protein diet. People who follow a ketogenic diet limit their daily carbohydrate consumption to 20 to 50 grams. This causes your body to enter a metabolic condition known as ketosis, where it burns fat for fuel instead of carbohydrates. This procedure converts dietary and bodily fat reserves into energy-producing ketones. This high-fat, moderate-protein, low-carbohydrate diet makes use of smart foods and helps people move away from processed food.

A ketogenic diet's goal is to keep the body in a state of ketosis so that you can lose weight or manage illnesses like Type 2 diabetes. A daily consumption of 20 to 50 grams of carbs is required to accomplish this. Since many modern meals contain carbohydrates, adhering to a ketogenic diet might be difficult, but there are numerous alternatives and solutions that can be used to prevent hunger.

The majority of the items on a ketogenic diet are unprocessed, whole foods that are high in fat and protein and low in carbohydrates. It has been discovered that eating mostly saturated and monounsaturated fats can help curb appetite and lower harmful cholesterol levels. Generally speaking, fruits and carbohydrates should be avoided, whereas foods like fish, meat, eggs, nuts, and dairy products are advised. During the transition, several ketogenic diet supplements may also be helpful.

In a medical context, the ketogenic diet is frequently employed, particularly as part of a treatment program for pediatric epilepsy. This diet can improve overall health since it makes the body use fat more effectively and makes it healthier in general. The ketogenic diet has been successful for those with diabetes as well. This is because these diets can aid in lowering cholesterol, blood glucose levels, and heart health.

Similarities between the Mediterranean and Ketogenic Diet

- **Sodium Consumption:** They both promote sodium intake. Mediterranean diet is rich in salt as a result of the oily dressings with increased amounts of salt and foods like cheese, olives, and anchovies. The Keto diet encourages the addition of salts to maintain electrolytes balance since the meals are low in salt.
- **Healthy food**: They both promote the consumption of protein and fresh vegetables and do not permit the use of chemicals, sugars, processed foods, or additives.
- **Health benefits:** There are many health benefits. Keto diet reduces the levels of total and LDL cholesterol, reduces the levels of triglycerides and increases the levels of HDL cholesterol which

could be beneficial for people with type 2 diabetes and in fighting some cancers. Mediterranean diet advocates the use of olive oil which has been discovered to reduce the risk of heart disease, death, and stroke.

Differences between the Ketogenic and Mediterranean Diet

- **Fat Consumption:** Mediterranean diet has a lower fat percentage than the ketogenic diet. Mediterranean diet also advocates the use of unsaturated like gotten from fish and oils whereas keto foods include both saturated and unsaturated oils.

- **Carbohydrate Consumption:** The Mediterranean diet advocates high carb, healthy fats, and no refined sugars whereas the ketogenic diet restricts carbs in every form.

Reasons for Integrating the Two Diet?

A ketogenic diet is one that derives the majority of its calories from dietary fat, contains only moderate levels of protein, and is very low in carbohydrates. This forces the body to go into a "fat burn" mode, relying on both dietary fat sources and stored body fat for daily fuel. The result is healthy weight management, blood sugar regulation, and improvements in many other health markers, such as blood pressure and cholesterol.

The Mediterranean Diet has been well studied for decades and is shown to have a positive impact on the health of those who follow it. While ketogenic dietary intervention is a relatively new science, I believe that the principles of a low-carb/high-fat approach to health, combined with the Mediterranean Diet's focus on heart-healthy fats and colorful, low-sugar plant foods, will become the gold standard among many healthcare providers working with individuals battling obesity, diabetes, and other chronic diseases.

The Ketogenic Mediterranean Diet

As the name suggests, the keto Mediterranean diet combines aspects of the Mediterranean diet with those of the keto diet. A diet that combines the high-fat, moderate-protein, and low-carb ratios of the keto diet with the heart-healthy and fiber-rich foods and healthy behaviors of the Mediterranean The goal is to optimize the health benefits achieved from both, including weight loss, brain and heart health, and lower blood sugar and cholesterol levels.

The keto Mediterranean diet includes many healthy options like fish, yogurt, vegetables, and olives while restricting certain carbs to increase metabolic activity and use ketones for energy. The best of both worlds, the Ketogenic Mediterranean Diet provides a whole host of health benefits. This diet focuses on clean eating, and by combining the two diets, we gain significant advantages and reduce the downsides associated with them individually.

Since We've got a basic understanding of how the Mediterranean and keto diets work individually, and we can understand how combining the best parts of each of these diets can create an almost perfect diet that is easy to follow and not heavily restrictive. The keto diet focuses on the macronutrients, while the Mediterranean diet ensures that the body receives the essential micronutrients.

The keto Mediterranean diet offers you the variety, flavor, and color of the Mediterranean diet while lowering your carbohydrate intake to help you lose weight and maintain that weight loss. All the ingredients and foods found in this diet are readily available. Unlike the traditional keto diet, there isn't a strict emphasis on counting your macronutrients. This makes it easier to stick with the diet for the long term. Unlike the keto diet, this hybrid is more inclusive, allowing for vegetarian and vegan plans.

Additionally, this combination has incredible health benefits. The keto Mediterranean diet may help control blood sugar and cholesterol levels, improve heart health, and lower your risk of inflammation. Not to mention, it promotes weight loss and improves the body's insulin sensitivity. Overall, the keto Mediterranean diet is a great choice for most who are looking for a healthier option that is feasible and flexible enough to work with their lifestyle.

Basics of the Keto Mediterranean Diet

Macronutrients: The Keto Mediterranean Diet is a high-fat, low-carbohydrate diet that includes healthy fats like olive oil, nuts, and avocados, as well as a moderate amount of protein. Macronutrients are the building blocks of a healthy diet, and they are necessary for many body functions. On the Keto Mediterranean Diet, macronutrients should be primarily sourced from healthy fats and protein, while carbohydrates should be limited; Magnesium:

Micronutrients: In the Keto-Mediterranean Diet, ensuring an adequate intake of micronutrients is crucial for maintaining overall health and well-being. While the diet emphasizes healthy fats, moderate protein, and low carbohydrates, it is essential to pay attention to essential vitamins and minerals to prevent nutrient deficiencies. Some key micronutrients include; Magnesium, potassium, calcium, vitamin (B-complex, C and D).

Principles of the Keto-Mediterranean Diet

- **Eat heavy meals followed by periods of no meals:** Although heavy meals provide the nutrients that are essential for maximum functioning while also ensuring that our weight is healthy, it is not advisable to eat them throughout the day. In actual Mediterranean diets, the Greeks are known to fast for about three months, this is responsible for the benefits of enhanced mental function, and improved heart function.

- **Eat more vegetables:** It is essential to include green leafy vegetables or cruciferous vegetables in each meal. They contain chemicals that improve immunity and fight cancer. Although the amount to be consumed depends on each person.

- **Opt for bitter foods more:** Similar to cruciferous and green vegetables, bitter foods like onions, bitter vegetables, bitter red wine, herbs, and garlic are rich in chemicals that improve the body's immunity. They prevent your taste buds from getting addicted to sweet and potentially unhealthy foods. Bitter foods also aid detoxification.

- **Minimize the quantity:** Most effective diets involve some form of carbohydrate restriction to lower blood glucose and suppress insulin while helping the body eliminate toxins. Although there is no standard value, nutritional ketosis needs less than 20 to 25grams each day while a very low or low carb diet is between 0 to 150grams each day. Sources of carbohydrates can include sweet potato, blackberries, and yucca. They are usually optimized faster after exercising.

- **Consume large amounts of fat:** A strict intermittent ketogenic diet is based on ample quantities of fat. The monounsaturated oil used in the Mediterranean diet is a good idea. Use rich cream, palm oil, macadamia, avocado and coconut oil with particularly for dressing, and with moderation.

- **Engage in routine exercises:** Engage in periods of exercises including resistance training and heavy weight lifting. It is important to know that the people of the Mediterranean engage in important routine exercise. They frequently take walks, engage in heavy lifting. Muscle contraction produces chemical substances that fight against cancer and inflammation.

What to Eat and Avoid

Despite an emphasis on legumes, wheat, grains, and certain vegetables, the Mediterranean diet is compatible with a low-carb and high-fat eating lifestyle. Here is the list of items you can eat and avoid in Mediterranean Ketogenic Diet.

What to Embrace

Although, the Keto-Mediterranean Diet combines the principles of Mediterranean and ketogenic diets, focusing on healthy fats, moderate protein, and low-carbohydrate options. Embrace the following are key foods to focus on in order to create a balanced and nutritious eating plan:

1. **Healthy Fats:** Use extra virgin olive oil, avocados, nuts, seeds, fatty fish, coconut oil, and grass-fed butter.

2. **Non-Starchy Vegetables:** Include leafy greens, cruciferous vegetables, bell peppers, zucchini, eggplant, cucumbers, onions, and garlic.

3. **Proteins:** Choose fatty fish, poultry, grass-fed meats, eggs, seafood, and plant-based proteins like tofu and tempeh.

4. **Low-Carb Fruits (in moderation):** Occasionally enjoy berries and avocados.

5. **Dairy (in moderation):** Opt for full-fat or low-carb options like Greek yogurt and cheese.

6. **Herbs and Spices:** Use a variety of herbs and spices to enhance flavor without adding extra carbohydrates.

7. **Beverages:** Stay hydrated with water, herbal teas, and black coffee. Moderate red wine consumption (if desired) is also associated with the Mediterranean diet.

Focus on whole, minimally processed foods and be mindful of individual carbohydrate tolerance. Consult with a healthcare professional or registered dietitian for personalized guidance and any specific health concerns or dietary restrictions.

What food needs to avoided

To maintain ketosis and follow the guidelines of the Keto-Mediterranean Diet, some high-carb and processed meals must be restricted or avoided. Consider the following important details:

1. **High-Carb Grains:** Steer clear of oats, quinoa, wheat, rice, and barley. Limit Starchy Vegetables: Eat less winter squash, maize, peas, and potatoes.

2. **Processed and Refined Foods:** Avoid processed meats, chips, sweetened beverages, and sugary snacks.

3. **High-Sugar Fruits:** Bananas, grapes, mangoes, pineapples, and dried fruits with added sugars should all be consumed in moderation.

4 **Sugary Sauces and Condiments**: Steer clear of ketchup, honey mustard, BBQ sauce, sweetened salad dressings, and teriyaki sauce.

5 **High-Carb Beverages:** Avoid sugar-laden energy drinks, ordinary soda, and fruit juices that have been sweetened.

6 **Limit or Avoid Legumes**: Limit your intake of kidney, black, lentil, and chickpeas.

You may maintain ketosis while consuming nutrient-dense, whole meals that adhere to the Keto-Mediterranean Diet's healthy principles by avoiding these foods. A trained dietician or healthcare provider can offer individualized advice and take into account particular dietary requirements or health issues.

Breakfast Recipes

Asparagus Frittata

Ingredients: *(Prep Time: 10 minutes Serves: 6 slices Cook Time: 20 minutes)*

- 1 Tbsp. unsalted butter
- 1 small white onion, chopped
- 2 garlic cloves, minced
- 4large whole eggs
- 1¼ cups heavy cream

- ¼ tsp dried oregano
- ⅛ tsp dried red pepper flakes
- Sea salt, to taste
- 4oz. feta cheese (crumbled)
- 10 oz. asparagus

Preparation Method:

1. Apply 325°Fheat to your oven and coat a 9-inch round baking pan lightly.
2. set a low heat to the pan to melt the butter. Add chopped onions and garlic. Cook for 5 minutes until translucent (not golden).
3. Mix-in the onion and garlic mixture to the baking pan. Sprinkle crumbled feta on the top. Arrange asparagus in a single layer in the pan.
4. Whisk eggs in a medium-sized bowl. Add the cream, oregano, red pepper flakes, and sea salt and whisk until fully incorporated.
5. Introduce the egg mixture on top of the pan's contents and bake.
6. Bake for 15–20 minutes until the frittata is set and lightly golden along the edges. Sprinkle with chopped fresh dill.

Nutrition per serve: *Calories: 305, Net Carbs: 4.4 g, Total Carbohydrates: 5.7 g, Total Fat: 28.4 g, Cholesterol 215 mg, Sodium 292 mg, Protein: 9.5 g, Fiber: 1.3 g, Sugar: 2.7 g*

Avocado Toast

Ingredients: *(Prep Time: 5 minutes Serves 2 Cook Time: 5 minutes)*

- 2 tablespoons ground flaxseed
- ½ teaspoon baking powder
- 2 large eggs
- 1 teaspoon salt
- ½ teaspoon freshly ground black pepper
- ½ teaspoon garlic powder, sesame seed, caraway seed or other dried herbs (optional)

- 3 tablespoons extra-virgin olive oil, divided
- 1 medium ripe avocado, peeled, pitted, and sliced
- 2 tablespoons chopped ripe tomato or salsa

Preparation Method:

1. Mix the flaxseed and baking powder in a small basin, making sure there are no lumps in the baking powder. Add the eggs, salt, pepper, and garlic powder (if using) and whisk well. Let sit for 2 minutes.
2. In a small non-stick skillet, apply heat to a 1 tablespoon olive oil over medium heat. Pour the egg mixture into the skillet and let cook undisturbed until the egg begins to set on bottom, 2 to 3 minutes.
3. Using a rubber spatula, scrape down the sides to allow uncooked egg to reach the bottom. Cook another 2 to 3 minutes.
4. Once almost set, flip like a pancake and allow the top to fully cook, another 1 to 2 minutes.
5. Take out of the pan and cool for a while. Slice into 2 pieces. Top each "toast" with avocado slices, additional salt and pepper, chopped tomato, and drizzle with the remaining 2 tablespoons olive oil.

Nutrition Per Serve: *Calories: 287, Total Fat: 25g, Total Carbs: 10g, Net Carbs: 3g, Fiber: 7g, Protein: 9g; Sodium: 1130mg Macros: Fat: 76%, Carbs: 12%, Protein: 12%*

Breakfast Bruschetta with Avocado and Salmon

Ingredients: *(Prep Time: 10 minutes Serves: 4)*

- 4 keto bread slices, grilled/toasted

For the toppings:

- 1 avocado, diced
- 8 oz. smoked salmon, sliced
- ½ red onion, diced
- 8 olives, pitted
- ½ cup fresh dill sprigs
- Ground white peppercorns
- 1 tsp. olive oil

Preparation Method:

1. Arrange all the toppings on the bread slices and sprinkle with ground pepper and olive oil. Linda's
2. Try bruschetta topped with liver pâté, or mashed avocado.

Nutrition per Serve: *Calories: 255, Net Carbs: 12 g, Total Carbs: 19.5 g, Total Fat: 15.2 g, Chol: 13 mg, Sodium 1344 mg, Protein: 14.5 g, Fiber: 7.5 g, Sugar: 1.2 g*

Blueberry Power Smoothie

Ingredients: *(Prep Time: 5 minutes Serves 1)*

- 1 cup unsweetened almond milk,
- ¼ cup frozen blueberries
- 2 tablespoons unsweetened almond butter
- 1 tablespoon ground flaxseed
- 1 tablespoon extra-virgin olive oil
- 1 to 2 teaspoons stevia (optional)
- ½ teaspoon vanilla extract
- ¼ teaspoon ground cinnamon

Preparation Method:

1. In a blender or a large wide-mouth jar, if using an immersion blender, combine the almond milk, blueberries, almond butter, flaxseed, olive oil, stevia (if using), vanilla, and cinnamon and blend until smooth and creamy, adding more almond milk to achieve your desired consistency.
2. Serve and enjoy.

Nutrition Per Serve: Calories: 460, Total Fat: 40g, Total Carbs: 20g, Net Carbs: 10g, Fiber: 10g, Protein: 9g; Sodium: 147mg Macros: Fat: 78%, Carbs: 17%, Protein: 5%

Caprese Omelet

Ingredients: *(Prep time: 5 minutes; Serves: 1 Cook time: 5 minutes)*

- 1/3 cup cherry tomatoes, halved
- 6 basil leaves, chopped
- 1/2 teaspoon sea salt
- 1/4 teaspoon cracked black pepper
- 1 tablespoon basil pesto, fresh
- 1 tablespoon olive oil and more for drizzling
- 3 eggs, pasture-raised
- 2 slices of fresh mozzarella cheese, full-fat
- 1 tablespoon grated Parmesan cheese, full-fat

Preparation Method:

1. Crack the eggs in a bowl and whisk until blended.
2. Place a small skillet pan over low heat, add oil and when hot, pour in eggs and bring the egg mixture to the center from pan from the sides with a spatula.
3. Then top one half of egg with half of the tomatoes, basil leaves, and cheeses and fold the other half of Caprese to cover this topping.
4. Cook omelet for 1 minute or until Caprese is set and then slide onto serving plate.
5. Drizzle Caprese with basil pesto and olive oil, top with remaining tomatoes and serve straightaway.

Nutrition Per Serve: *Calories: 533 Cal, Carbs: 4.9 g, Fat: 43.2 g, Protein: 30.8 g, Fiber: 1.1 g.*

Chicken Casserole

Ingredients: *(Prep Time: 15 minutes Serves: 8 Cook Time: 55 minutes)*

- 1 lb. turkey/chicken fillets, diced
- 1 white onion, chopped
- 10 oz. broccoli florets
- 1 cup whole milk
- 6 slices of keto bread, cut into bite-sized pieces
- 1 cup bell peppers, chopped
- 1 can (14 oz.) artichoke hearts, drained
- ½ cup feta cheese, crumbled
- 8 whole eggs
- ½ tsp. kosher salt
- 2 tbsp. olive oil

Preparation Method:

1. Apply 350°F heat to your oven.
2. Heat olive oil in a large skillet over medium-high heat. Add chicken pieces and cook for 8 minutes, stirring occasionally.
3. Add chopped onion and salt to the skillet. Cook for an additional 5 minutes. In a container, whisk gently the milk and eggs.

4. Spray a baking dish with cooking spray. Transfer the ingredients from the skillet to the baking dish. Add chopped vegetables, crumbled feta, and bread pieces. Pour the milk-egg mixture over them.
5. Allow the casserole to Bake in the heated oven for 35–45 minutes. Remove from the oven and let it sit for 10 minutes before serving.

Nutrition Per Serve: *Calories: 311, Net Carbs: 6.5 g, Total Carbohydrates: 12 g, Total Fat: 15.1 g, Cholesterol 223 mg, Sodium 353 mg, Protein: 29.5 g, Fiber: 5.5 g, Sugar: 3.7 g*

Egg Muffins

Ingredients: *(Prep Time: 10 minutes Serves: 8 Cook Time: 20 minutes)*

- 6 large eggs
- 2 Tbsp. heavy cream
- 2 cups broccoli florets
- 1 small yellow onion, chopped
- 3 oz. turkey/chicken fillets, cooked and chopped
- 4 oz. feta, crumbled
- ¼ tsp. smoked paprika
- kosher salt as required
- black pepper as needed

Preparation Method:

1. Whisk eggs, heavy cream, salt, pepper, and paprika together in a bowl. Combine the egg mixture with the remaining ingredients.
2. Apply 350°F heat to your oven.
3. Spray muffin molds with olive oil. Pour the muffin mixture into the molds.
4. Bake for 15–20 minutes or until set. Let them cool slightly before serving.

Nutrition Per Serve: *Calories: 134, Net Carbs: 2.5 g, Total Carbohydrates: 3.3 g, Total Fat: 8.7 g, Cholesterol 166 mg, Sodium 224 mg, Protein: 10.5 g, Fiber: 0.8 g, Sugar: 1.7 g*

Egg Salad Lettuce Wraps

Ingredients: *(Prep time: 10 minutes Serves: 4 Cook time: 10 minutes)*

- 6 hard-boiled eggs, chopped
- 1/4 cup diced cucumber
- 1/4 cup diced red bell pepper
- 1/4 cup diced red onion
- 1/4 cup chopped Kalamata olives
- 2 tablespoons chopped fresh parsley
- 2 tablespoons chopped fresh dill
- 1/4 cup mayonnaise
- 1 tablespoon lemon juice
- Salt and pepper to taste
- 8 large lettuce leaves

Preparation Method:

1. In a mixing bowl, combine the chopped hard-boiled eggs, cucumber, red bell pepper, red onion, Kalamata olives, parsley, and dill.
2. In a separate small bowl, whisk together the mayonnaise and lemon juice. Season with salt and pepper to taste.
3. Pour the mayonnaise mixture over the egg mixture and gently toss until well combined. Place a scoop of the egg salad onto each lettuce leaf.
4. Fold the sides of the lettuce leaf inward and roll it up tightly to form a wrap. Repeat with the remaining lettuce leaves and egg salad.
5. Serve the Mediterranean Egg Salad Lettuce Wraps immediately.

Nutrition Per Serve: *Calories: 256 Protein: 14g Carbohydrates: 5g Fat: 20g Fiber: 2g Cholesterol: 378mg Sodium: 419mg Potassium: 252mg*

French Gratin with Cheese Crust

Ingredients: *(Prep Time: 15 minutes Serves: 4 Cook Time: 1 hour)*

- 8 oz. chicken fillets, chunks
- 7 oz. mushrooms, diced
- 1 white onion, chopped
- 8 oz. broccoli florets/Brussels sprouts/artichoke
- 1 cup whole milk

- ½ cup feta cheese, crumbled
- 8 whole eggs
- 1 cup parmesan/Gruyere, shredded
- ½ tsp. salt
- 2 tbsp. olive oil
- Oil spray

Preparation Method:

1. Preheat your oven to 350°F (180°C). Heat olive oil in a large skillet over medium-high heat.
2. Add chicken pieces and cook for 8 minutes, stirring occasionally. Add chopped onion, diced mushrooms, and salt to the skillet. Allow the mix cook for approximately 5 minutes, stirring occasionally, until tender.
3. Lightly beat eggs and milk together in a bowl. Grease a baking dish with oil spray.
4. Transfer the ingredients from the skillet to the baking dish and mix in vegetables and crumbled feta cheese. introduce the milk and egg mix. Sprinkle with shredded Parmesan.
5. Bake the gratin in the preheated oven for 35–45 minutes. Serve with dinner rolls and fresh summer salad.

Nutrition Per Serve: *Calories: 518, Net Carbs: 10.3 g, Total Carbs: 12.9 g, Total Fat: 34.1 g, Chol: 416 mg, Sodium 623 mg, Protein: 42.5 g, Fiber: 2.6 g, Sugar: 7.7 g*

Keto Greek Yogurt Smoothie with Cucumber and Mint

Ingredients: (*Prep time: 5 minutes Serves: 2 Cook time: 0 minutes*)

- 1 cup Greek yogurt
- 1 cup cucumber, peeled and chopped
- 1/2 cup fresh mint leaves

- 1/2 cup unsweetened almond milk
- 1 tablespoon lemon juice

Optionals

- 1 tablespoon Erythritol or preferred keto-friendly sweetener

- Ice cubes

Preparation Method:

1. In a blender, combine the Greek yogurt, cucumber, mint leaves, almond milk, lemon juice, and sweetener (if using).
2. Blend until smooth and creamy. If desired, add ice cubes and blend again until the smoothie reaches your desired consistency.
3. Distribute the smoothie among glasses and top with more mint if desired.

Nutrition Per Serve: *Calories: 105 Protein: 10g Carbohydrates: 6g Fat: 4g Fiber: 1g Cholesterol: 5mg Sodium: 73mg Potassium: 296mg*

Mushroom Frittata with Parmesan

Ingredients: *(Prep Time: 10 minutes Serves: 4 /Cook Time: 20 minutes)*

- 4 medium eggs
- 3 Tbsp. heavy cream
- ⅓ cup feta cheese, crumbled
- 4 cremini mushrooms, sliced
- 2 white onions, diced

- 4 Tbsp. baby spinach, chopped
- 2 scallions, roughly chopped
- ⅓ cup parmesan, grated
- Sea salt as required
- ground black peppercorns, as needed

Preparation Method:

1. Apply 400°F heat to your oven.
2. Whisk heavy cream together with eggs, salt, and pepper. Mix in vegetables and feta cheese.
3. Spray a baking pan with olive oil. Pour the frittata mixture into the baking pan and sprinkle with grated Parmesan.
4. Allow to cook in the heated oven between the range of 15–20 minutes. Serve with crispy keto ciabatta.

Nutrition Per Serve: *Calories: 181, Net Carbs: 6.4 g, Total Carbohydrates: 7.9 g, Total Fat: 12.4 g, Cholesterol 194 mg, Sodium 258 mg, Protein: 10.5 g, Fiber: 1.5 g, Sugar: 3.7 g*

Olive & Herb Focaccia

Ingredients: *(Prep time: 10 minutes; Serves: 4 Cook time: 15 minutes)*

- 1/4 cup sliced Kalamata olives, fresh
- 1/3 cup and 1 tablespoon coconut flour
- 2 1/2 tablespoons psyllium husks
- 1 teaspoon baking powder
- 1/2 teaspoon salt

- 1 tablespoon minced fresh rosemary
- 1 tablespoon minced fresh sage
- 2 tablespoons olive oil
- 4 eggs, pasture-raised
- 2 tablespoons Greek yogurt

Preparation Method:

1. Apply 375 degrees F to your oven and let preheat. In the meantime, crack eggs in a bowl, add yogurt and whisk until combined.
2. Place flour in another bowl, add psyllium husks, baking powder, and salt and mix til properly mixed. Add egg mixture and stir well until soft dough comes together.
3. Take a baking sheet, line with parchment paper, place dough on it and shape into a ½-inch thick rectangle.
4. Place a small saucepan over low heat, add salt, minced rosemary, and sage, 1 tablespoon olive oil and allow to cook for maximum 2 minutes or until fragrant.
5. Spoon this mixture over dough, then scatter with olive and drizzle with remaining oil and place baking tray into the heated oven.
6. Bake Focaccia for 15 minutes or until top is nicely golden brown and cooked through. When done, slice to serve.

Nutrition Per Serve: *Calories: 144 Cal, Carbs: 4.8 g, Fat: 10.9 g, Protein: 6.6 g, Fiber: 3 g.*

Pesto Scrambled Eggs

Ingredients: *(Prep time: 5 minutes; Serves: 1 Cook time: 5 minutes)*

- 3 eggs, pasture-raised
- ½ teaspoon salt
- ½ teaspoon cracked black pepper
- 1 tablespoon unsalted butter

- 1 tablespoon olive oil
- 1 tablespoon basil pesto, fresh
- 2 tablespoons soured cream, full-fat

Preparation Method:

1. Whisk together the cracked eggs, salt, and black pepper in a bowl.
2. Place a medium skillet pan over low heat, pour in egg mixture, add butter and oil and stir well with a whisker.
3. Then whisk in pesto and cook for 1 to 2 minutes or until creamy scrambled eggs come together.
4. Remove pan from heat, introduce the sour cream until well mixed and spoon scrambled eggs into serving plate.
5. Serve straightaway.

Nutrition Per Serve: *Calories: 467 Cal, Carbs: 3.3 g, Fat: 41.5 g, Protein: 20.4 g, Fiber: 0.7 g.*

Savory Pancake

Ingredients: *(Prep time: 5 minutes; Serves: 1 Cook time: 10 minutes)*

- 2 tablespoons coconut flour
- 2 tablespoons chopped chives
- ½ teaspoon salt
- ¼ teaspoon cracked black pepper
- 1/4 teaspoon apple cider vinegar
- 1 tablespoon olive oil
- 3 eggs, pasture-raised
- 1/2 cup grated Parmesan cheese, full-fat

Preparation Method:

1. First, position your egg whites in a container and the yolks in another. Into egg whites, add vinegar and beat using a stand mixer until stiff peaks forms.
2. Then fold in egg yolks, cheese, flour, chives, salt and black pepper with a whisker. Set a moderate heat to a small skillet, and add oil and when hot, pour in pancake mixture.
3. Cook for 3 minutes or until bottom sets and bubbles appear on top.
4. Turn on broiler, place pan containing pancake into the broiler and allow it cook for maximum 5 minutes or until top is nicely golden brown.
5. When done, slide pancake to a serving plate and serve.

Nutrition Per Serve: *Calories: 294 Cal, Carbs: 3.8 g, Fat: 21.7 g, Protein: 19 g, Fiber: 1.5 g.*

Spiced Orange-Pistachio Smoothie

Ingredients (Prep Time: 5 minutes: Serves 1 Cook Time: 0 minutes)

- ½ cup plain whole-milk Greek yogurt
- ½ cup unsweetened almond milk
- Juice of 1 clementine or ½ orange
- 1 tablespoon extra-virgin olive oil
- 1 tablespoon shelled pistachios, coarsely chopped
- 1 to 2 teaspoons monk fruit extract or stevia (optional)
- ¼ to ½ teaspoon ground allspice
- ¼ teaspoon ground cinnamon
- ¼ teaspoon vanilla extract

Preparation Method:

1. In a blender or a large wide-mouth jar, if using an immersion blender, combine the yogurt, ½ cup almond milk, clementine zest and juice, olive oil, pistachios, monk fruit extract (if using), allspice, cinnamon, and vanilla and pulse until smooth and creamy, adding more almond milk to achieve your desired consistency.

Nutrition Per Serve: *Calories: 264, Total Fat: 22g, Total Carbs: 12g, Net Carbs: 10g, Fiber: 2g, Protein: 6g; Sodium: 127mg*

Spinach Wrap

Ingredients: *(Prep Time: 5 minutes Serves: 1 Cook Time: 5 minutes)*

- 2 Tbsp. flaxseed meal
- 1 whole egg
- ¼ cup fresh spinach
- ¼ tsp. garlic powder
- ¼ tsp. baking powder
- 1 Tbsp. water

Preparation Method:

1. Grease an 8-inch glass baking dish with oil spray. In a food processor, combine egg, spinach, water, flaxseed meal, garlic powder, and baking powder.
2. Transfer the mixture to the baking dish, ensuring a uniform and smooth texture. Place the dish in the microwave and microwave on high for 3–4 minutes.
3. Remove from the oven and let it stand for 2 minutes.
4. Serve with scrambled egg and avocado, or choose your favorite filling.

Nutrition Per Serve: *Calories: 144, Net Carbs: 1.8 g, Total Carbohydrates: 6 g, Total Fat: 8.9 g, Cholesterol 164 mg, Sodium 79 mg, Protein: 8.7 g, Fiber: 4.2 g, Sugar: 0.8 g*

Spinach and Feta Crustless Quiche

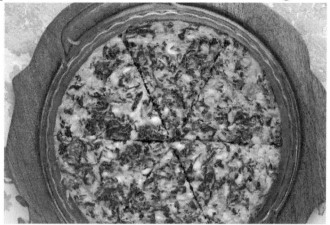

Ingredients: *(Prep time: 15 minutes Serves: 4 Cook time: 30 minutes)*

- 1 tablespoon olive oil
- 1 small onion, diced
- 2 garlic cloves, minced
- 4 cups fresh spinach leaves
- 1/2 cup crumbled feta cheese

- 4 large eggs
- 1/2 cup heavy cream
- 1/4 teaspoon dried oregano
- Salt and black pepper to taste
- optional: cherry tomatoes, sliced

Preparation Method:

1. Apply 375°F heat to the oven and coat a 9-inch pie dish lightly with olive oil. Set a moderate heat to the olive oil in a skillet. Add the diced onion and minced garlic. Sauté until the onion becomes translucent.
2. introduce the fresh spinach leaves into the skillet and allow to cook until it wilted, about 2-3 minutes.
3. Spread the cooked spinach equally in the prepared pie dish. Crumble the feta cheese and toss it with the spinach.
4. In a distinct container, whisk together the eggs, heavy cream, dried oregano, salt, and black pepper. Top the spinach and feta with the egg mixture.
5. If desired, arrange sliced cherry tomatoes on top for added flavor and visual appeal. Allow to bake in the heated oven at range of 25-30 minutes, or until the quiche is set and the top is golden brown.
6. Remove from the oven and let it cool for a few minutes before serving.

Nutrition per serve: *Calories: 252 Protein: 13g Carbohydrates: 5g Fat: 20g Fiber: 1g Cholesterol: 240mg Sodium: 317mg Potassium: 351mg*

Sicilian Caponata

Ingredients: *(Prep Time: 10 minutes Serves: 4 Cook Time: 25 minutes)*

- 1 eggplant, cubed
- 1 red onion, chopped
- 1 bell pepper, chopped
- 2 medium tomatoes, chopped
- 1 celery stalk, diced
- Sea salt, black pepper
- 2 Tbsp. capers

- 1 Tbsp. pine nuts
- 3 Tbsp. olives, diced
- ¼ tsp. red pepper flakes
- ¼ cup red wine vinegar
- ¼ cup fresh Italian herbs, chopped
- Olive oil

Preparation Method:

1. Apply 400°F heat to your oven. Season eggplant cubes with salt and pepper and drizzle with some olive oil.
2. Roast in the heated oven for approximately 25 minutes until golden brown, tossing twice during the process. Set heat to a tablespoon of olive oil in a your pan and add chopped onion, bell peppers, celery, salt, and pepper. Cook for 5 minutes until softened.
3. Add tomatoes, capers, olives, pine nuts, vinegar, and red pepper flakes. Cook, while stirring, for an additional 7–8 minutes.
4. Add the roasted eggplant and chopped herbs and cook for another 5 minutes. Serve as a topping over a keto baguette or ciabatta.

Nutrition Per Serve: *Calories: 160, Net Carbs: 7.8 g, Total Carbohydrates: 16 g, Total Fat: 9.7 g, Cholesterol 0 mg, Sodium 195 mg, Protein: 3.5 g, Fiber: 8.2 g, Sugar: 9.7 g*

Skewers with Halloumi Cheese and Cherry Tomatoes

Ingredients: (*Prep time: 15 minutes Serves: 4 Cook time: 10 minutes*)

- 8 wooden skewers
- 8 ounces' halloumi cheese, cubed
- 16 cherry tomatoes
- 1 tablespoon extra-virgin olive oil
- 1 teaspoon dried oregano
- Salt and pepper, to taste
- Fresh basil leaves, for garnish

Preparation Method:

1. Preheat the grill or grill pan over medium heat. Soak the wooden skewers in water for about 10 minutes to prevent them from burning.
2. Thread the halloumi cheese cubes and cherry tomatoes onto the skewers, alternating between them.
3. Incorporate the extra virgin olive oil, dried oregano, salt, and pepper in a small container and swirl it together.
4. Coat the skewers evenly with the olive oil mixture and brush it on. Cook the kebabs approximately 3–4 minutes on each side, or until the cheese is gently browned and the tomatoes are softened, on a grill or grill pan. Take the skewers from the grill and let them cool for a moment.
5. Garnish with fresh basil leaves. Serve the Mediterranean breakfast skewers as a delicious and protein-packed breakfast option.

Nutrition Per Serve: *Calories: 246 Protein: 16g Carbohydrates: 6g Fat: 18g Fiber: 1g Cholesterol: 54mg Sodium: 698mg Potassium: 200mg*

Smoked Salmon and Cream Cheese Rolls

Ingredients: *(Prep time: 10 minutes Serves: 4 Cook time: 0 minutes)*

- 8 slices smoked salmon
- 4 ounces' cream cheese, softened
- 1/4 cup chopped Kalamata olives
- 2 tablespoons chopped fresh dill
- 1 tablespoon capers
- 1 tablespoon lemon juice
- Salt and black pepper to taste

Preparation Method:

1. Lay the smoked salmon slices on a clean surface.
2. In a small container, integrate the softened cream cheese, chopped Kalamata olives, chopped fresh dill, capers, lemon juice, salt, and black pepper. Mix well until all ingredients are incorporated.
3. Put a small amount of the cream cheese mix on every piece of smoked salmon. Roll up the salmon slices tightly, starting from one end.
4. Once rolled, slice each roll into bite-sized pieces. Arrange the salmon roll-ups on a serving platter.
5. Serve immediately and enjoy the Mediterranean Smoked Salmon and Cream Cheese Roll-Ups as an appetizer or snack.

Nutrition Per Serve: *Calories: 162 Protein: 12g Carbohydrates: 2g Fat: 12g Fiber: 0g Cholesterol: 42mg Sodium: 530mg Potassium: 224mg*

Lunch Recipes

Asparagus Salmon Fillets

Ingredients: *(Prep Time: 10 minutes Serves: 2 Cook Time: 20 minutes)*

- 1 teaspoon olive oil
- 4 asparagus stalks
- 2 salmon fillets
- ¼ cup butter
- ¼ cup champagne
- Salt and freshly ground black pepper, to taste

Preparation Method:

1. Preheat the oven to 355 degrees and grease a baking dish. Put all the ingredients in a bowl and mix well.
2. Put this mixture in the baking dish and transfer it to the oven.
3. Bake for about 20 minutes and dish out.
4. Place the salmon fillets in a dish and set them aside to cool for meal prepping. Divide it into 2 containers and close the lid.
5. Refrigerate for 1 day and reheat in microwave before serving.

Nutrition Per Serve: *Calories: 475 Carbs: 1.1g Protein: 35.2g Fat: 36.8g Sugar: 0.5g Sodium: 242mg*

Bacon, Lettuce, and Tomato Stuffed Avocado

Ingredients: *(Prep Time: 10 minutes Serves: 2 Cook Time: 5 minutes)*

- 2 medium avocados, halved, pitted
- ½ cup halved grape tomatoes
- 1 teaspoon lime juice
- ¼ teaspoon sea salt or to taste

- 2 slices bacon
- ½ cup chopped Romaine lettuce
- ¼ teaspoon garlic powder
- ⅛ teaspoon pepper

Preparation Method:

1. Add bacon into a skillet and place the skillet over medium heat.
2. Cook until crisp. Remove the bacon from the pan and place it on a plate lined with paper towels.
3. Scoop out some flesh from the avocado halves and put them into a bowl. Place the avocado halves on a serving platter.
4. Mash the scooped avocado, adding garlic powder, lime juice, and salt using a fork. Taste a bit and add more salt and lime juice if required.
5. Add in the lettuce and grape tomatoes.
6. Chop bacon into pieces on cooling. Add bacon to the bowl of mashed avocado and mix well. Fill this mixture into the avocado halves.

Nutrition per serve: *Calories: 186 Fat: 16 g Total Carbohydrate: 10 g Net Carbohydrate: 3 g Fiber: 7 g Protein: 4 g (2 stuffed avocado halves)*

Caprese Stuffed Portobello Mushrooms

Ingredients: *(Prep Time: 5 minutes Serves: 2 Cook Time: 15 minutes)*

- 1 ½ tablespoons extra-virgin olive oil, divided
- ¼ teaspoon salt, divided
- 2 large *(3.5 ounces each)* portobello mushrooms
- ¼ cup fresh mozzarella pearls, drained
- 1 teaspoon balsamic vinegar
- 2 small cloves garlic, minced
- ¼ teaspoon pepper, divided
- ½ cup halved cherry tomatoes
- ¼ cup thinly sliced fresh basil leaves

Preparation Method:

1. Preheat the oven to 400°F. Add garlic, 1 tablespoon of oil, and half of each salt and pepper into a small bowl and mix well. Brush this mixture over the mushrooms and place them on a baking sheet.
2. Place the baking sheet in the oven and set the timer for about 10 minutes or until nearly soft but not completely soft.
3. Add mozzarella, tomatoes, basil, remaining salt, oil, and pepper into a bowl and mix well.
4. Stuff this mixture into the mushroom caps. Continue baking until the cheese melts and the tomatoes are slightly soft. Drizzle balsamic vinegar on top and serve.

Nutrition Per Serve: *Calories: 186 Fat: 16 g Total Carbohydrate: 6.3 g Net Carbohydrate: g Fiber: 1.9 g Protein: g (1 stuffed mushroom)*

Club Sandwich

Ingredients: *(Prep Time: 5 minutes Serve: 1)*

- 3 iceberg lettuce leaves
- 2 ounces' deli ham, thinly sliced
- 1-ounce cheddar cheese, thinly sliced
- 1 slice of cooked bacon
- 1 ½ teaspoon keto-friendly mayonnaise, divided
- 3 ounces' deli turkey, thinly sliced
- 1 thin round tomato slice (3 inches in diameter)

Preparation Method:

1. Place a lettuce leaf on a plate. Spread ½ teaspoon of the mayonnaise over the leaf.
2. Place a slice of cheese over the lettuce. Next, place the ham slices. Place another leaf of lettuce over the ham. Spread ½ teaspoon of mayonnaise over the lettuce.
3. Now place bacon, tomato slices, cheese, and turkey slices.
4. Spread ½ teaspoon mayonnaise over the turkey.
5. Place the remaining lettuce leaf on top. Cut into two halves. Insert a toothpick in each half and serve.

Nutrition Per Serve: *Calories: 413 Fat: 28 g Total Carbohydrate: 5 g Net Carbohydrate: 4 g Fiber: 1 g Protein: 35 g*

Creamy Chicken

Ingredients: *(Prep Time: 12 minutes Serves: 2 Cook Time: 13 minutes)*

½ small onion, chopped

¼ cup mushrooms

¼ cup sour cream

½ pound chicken breasts

1 tablespoon butter

Preparation Method:

1. Heat butter in a skillet and add onions and mushrooms.
2. Sauté for about 5 minutes and add chicken breasts and salt. Secure the lid and cook for about 5 more minutes.
3. Add sour cream and cook for about 3 minutes. Open the lid and dish it out in a bowl to serve immediately.
4. Transfer the creamy chicken breasts to a dish and set aside to cool for meal prepping.
5. Divide them into 2 containers and cover their lid. Refrigerate for 2-3 days and reheat in microwave before serving.

Nutrition Per Serve: *Calories: 335 Carbs: 2.9g Protein: 34g Fat: 20.2g Sugar: 0.8g Sodium: 154mg*

Crispy Baked Chicken

Ingredients: *(Prep Time: 30 minutes Serves: 2 Cook Time: 10 minutes)*

- 2 chicken breasts, skinless and boneless
- 2 tablespoons butter
- ¼ teaspoon turmeric powder
- Salt and black pepper, to taste
- ¼ cup sour cream

Preparation Method:

1. Preheat the oven to 360 degrees and grease a baking dish with butter.
2. Season the chicken with turmeric powder, salt, and black pepper in a bowl.
3. Put the chicken on the baking dish and transfer it to the oven.
4. Bake for about 10 minutes and dish out to serve topped with sour cream.

5. Transfer the chicken to a bowl and set aside to cool for meal prepping.
6. Divide it into 2 containers and cover the containers. Refrigerate for up to 2 days and reheat in microwave before serving.

Nutrition Per Serve: Calories: 304 Carbs: 1.4g Protein: 26.1g Fat: 21.6g Sugar: 0.1g Sodium: 137mg

Crispy Ginger Mackerel Lunch Bowls

Ingredients: *(Prep Time: 15 minutes Serves: 2 Cook Time: 15 minutes)*

Ginger Thai-Hini Dressing

- 1 tablespoon grated fresh ginger
- 1 tablespoon fresh lime or lemon juice
- 2 tablespoons extra-virgin olive oil
- 2 tablespoons tahini
- 1 clove garlic, minced

Mackerel

2 mackerel fillets Pinch of salt and black pepper

1 tablespoon (15 ml) extra-virgin avocado oil or ghee

To Assemble

- 16 to 20 spears asparagus
- 1 small (3.5 oz.) bok choy, halved
- 1 tablespoon extra-virgin olive oil
- ½ pack (6 oz.) kelp noodles, drained
- ¼ cup (1.2 oz.) macadamia nuts, roughly chopped
- 1 small (0.5 oz.) chile pepper, sliced
- 1 t tablespoon (0.2 oz.) chopped fresh cilantro or parsley

Preparation Method:

1. Place the dressing ingredients in a bowl and mix to combine. If the dressing is too thick, add a dash of water.

41

2. Cut 2 or 3 diagonal slits in the skin of the mackerel and season with salt and pepper on both sides. Heat a skillet greased with the avocado oil over medium heat. Add the mackerel fillets and cook for 2 to 3 minutes per side. Remove from the heat and set aside.

3. Place the asparagus and the bok choy in a steamer (or a saucepan with a steamer colander inside) and fill with about 1 cup (240 ml) of water and bring to a boil. Cover with a lid and steam for 3 to 5 minutes, until crisp-tender. Remove the lid and let the steam escape.

4. Divide the steamed veggies between two bowls, drizzle with the olive oil, and season with salt and pepper. Add the prepared kelp noodles and top with the mackerel.

5. Drizzle with the dressing and top with the macadamias, chile pepper, and cilantro. Eat warm or refrigerate for up to 1 day.

Nutrition Per Serve: *Total carbs: 13.3 g Fiber: 6.5 g Net Carbs: 6.8 g Protein: 30.5 g Fat: 66.2 g (of which saturated: 11 g) Calories: 751 kcal (1 Bowl)*

Feta Cheese Stuffed Bell Peppers

Ingredients: *(Prep Time: 10 minutes Serves: 4 Cook Time: 20 minutes)*

- 4 green bell peppers, halved lengthwise, deseeded
- 20 green olives, pitted, chopped
- 1 tablespoon dried mint leaves
- 22 ounces of feta cheese
- 4 eggs

- 2 teaspoons hot sauce
- 4 tablespoons olive oil (To serve)
- 2 ounces of leafy greens of your choice (To serve)
- ¼ teaspoon sea salt (To serve)

Preparation Method:

1. Preheat the oven to 400°F.
2. Add feta, hot sauce, olives, mint, and eggs into a bowl and stir until well combined.
3. Fill the mixture into the bell pepper halves and put them in a baking dish. Place the baking dish in the oven and set the timer for 20 minutes or until the top is golden brown.

4. To assemble: Place greens with assaulted color in a bowl. Add salt and oil and toss well.
5. Divide the greens into four plates. Place two bell pepper halves on each plate and serve.

Nutrition Per Serve: *Calories: 640 Fat: 53.34 g Total Carbohydrate: 12.63 g Net Carbohydrate: 11.23 g Fiber: 1.4 g Protein: 29.04 g (2 stuffed halves)*

Greek Cauliflower Rice

Ingredients: *(Prep Time: 15 minutes Serves: 4 Cook Time: 35 minutes)*

- ½ small head cauliflower, grated
- ¼ cup diced onion
- ½ cup halved grape tomatoes
- ¼ cup halved kalamata olives
- ⅛ cup chopped fresh parsley
- ⅛ cup fine sea salt
- ⅛ cup chopped walnuts (toasting is optional)

- 1 tablespoon olive oil, divided
- ½ tablespoon minced garlic
- ¼ cup chopped English cucumber
- ¼ cup crumbled feta cheese
- Zest of ½ lemon, grated
- Juice of ½ lemon, grated
- Pepper to taste

Preparation Method:

1. Pour ½ tablespoon oil into a non-stick pan and let it heat over medium-high heat.
2. When the oil is hot, add onion and garlic and cook until the onion is translucent.
3. Add cauliflower and cook until tender. Stir occasionally. Turn off the heat.
4. Remove the cauliflower from the pan and place it in a bowl. Add olives, tomatoes, parsley, lemon juice, lemon zest, salt, pepper, and cucumber, and toss well.
5. Add walnuts and remaining oil just before serving. Toss well and serve.

Nutrition Per Serve: *Calories: 109 Fat: 9 g Total Carbohydrate: 6 g Net Carbohydrate: 4 g Fiber: 2 g Protein: 3 g (¼ the recipe)*

Honey Glazed Chicken Drumsticks

Ingredients: *(Prep Time: 10 minutes Serves: 2 Cook Time: 20 minutes)*

- ½ tablespoon fresh thyme, minced
- 1/8 cup Dijon mustard
- ½ tablespoon fresh rosemary, minced
- ½ tablespoon honey
- 2 chicken drumsticks
- 1 tablespoon olive oil
- Salt and black pepper, to taste

Preparation Method:

1. Preheat the oven at 325 degrees and grease a baking dish.
2. Combine all the ingredients in a bowl except the drumsticks and mix well.
3. Add drumsticks and coat generously with the mixture. Cover and refrigerate to marinate overnight.
4. Place the drumsticks in the baking dish and transfer them to the oven. Cook for about 20 minutes and dish out to immediately serve.
5. Place chicken drumsticks in a dish and set them aside to cool for meal prepping. Divide it into 2 containers and cover them.
6. Refrigerate for about 3 days and reheat in microwave before serving.

Nutrition Per Serve: *Calories: 301 Carbs: 6g Fats: 19.7g Proteins: 4.5g Sugar: 4.5g Sodium: 316mg*

Lemongrass Prawns

Ingredients: *(Prep Time: 10 minutes Serves: 2 Cook Time: 15 minutes)*

- ½ red chili pepper, seeded and chopped
- 2 lemongrass stalks
- ½ pound prawns, deveined and peeled
- 6 tablespoons butter
- ¼ teaspoon smoked paprika

Preparation Method:

1. Preheat the oven to 390 degrees and grease a baking dish. Mix together red chili pepper, butter, smoked paprika, and prawns in a bowl.
2. Marinate for about 2 hours and then thread the prawns on the lemongrass stalks.
3. Arrange the threaded prawns on the baking dish and transfer them to the oven.
4. Bake for about 15 minutes and dish out to serve immediately. Place the prawns in a dish and set them aside to cool for meal prepping.
5. Divide it into 2 containers and close the lid. Refrigerate for about 4 days and reheat in microwave before serving.

Nutrition Per Serve: Calories: 322 Carbs: 3.8g Protein: 34.8g Fat: 18g Sugar: 0.1g Sodium: 478mg

Paprika Butter Shrimp

Ingredients: *(Prep Time: 15 minutes Serves: 2 Cook Time: 15 minutes)*

- ¼ tablespoon smoked paprika
- 1/8 cup sour cream
- ½ pound shrimp
- 1/8 cup butter
- Salt and black pepper, to taste

Preparation Method:

1. Preheat the oven to 390 degrees and grease a baking dish.
2. Mix together all the ingredients in a large bowl and transfer them into the baking dish.
3. Place in the oven and bake for about 15 minutes.
4. Place paprika shrimp in a dish and set aside to cool for meal prepping. Divide it into 2 containers and cover the lid.
5. Refrigerate for 1-2 days and reheat in microwave before serving.

Nutrition Per Serve: *Calories: 330 Carbs: 1.5g Protein: 32.6g Fat: 21.5g Sugar: 0.2g Sodium: 458mg*

Roasted Garlic Shrimp

Ingredients: *(Prep Time: 5 minutes Serves: 4 Cook Time: 10 minutes)*

- 1 lb. raw shrimp
- 2 garlic cloves, minced
- ½ tsp. anise seeds
- 1 Tbsp. olive oil
- kosher salt, and lemon pepper
- 2 Tbsp. fresh parsley, finely chopped
- 4 lemon wedges for sprinkling

Preparation Method:

1 Preheat your oven to 400°F (205°C).
2 Toss shrimp with minced garlic, anise seeds, olive oil, salt, and pepper.
3 Arrange shrimp on a baking sheet.
4 Roast for 8–10 minutes, depending on the size of the shrimp.
5 Sprinkle with chopped parsley and serve with lemon wedges.

Nutrition Per Serve: *Calories: 170, Net Carbs: 2.8 g, Total Carbohydrates: 3.1 g, Total Fat: 5.1 g, Cholesterol 237 mg, Sodium 276 mg, Protein: 25.9 g, Fiber: .0.3 g, Sugar: 0.2 g*

Salmon Burgers

Ingredients: *(Prep Time: 17 minutes Serves: 2 Cook Time: 3 minutes)*

- 1 tablespoon sugar-free ranch dressing
- ½-ounce smoked salmon, chopped roughly
- ½ tablespoon fresh parsley, chopped
- ½ tablespoon avocado oil
- 1 small egg
- 4-ounce pink salmon, drained and bones removed
- 1/8 cup almond flour
- ¼ teaspoon Cajun seasoning

Preparation Method:

1. Mix together all the ingredients in a bowl and stir well.
2. Make patties from this mixture and set them aside.
3. Heat a skillet over medium heat and add patties. Cook for about 3 minutes per side and dish out to serve.

4. You can store the raw patties in the freezer for about 3 weeks for meal prepping.
5. Place patties in a container and place parchment paper in between the patties to avoid stickiness.

Nutrition Per Serve: *Calories: 59 Fat: 12.7g Carbs: 2.4g Protein: 6.3g Sugar: 0.7g Sodium: 25mg*

Shrimp Scampi Zoodles

Ingredients: *(Prep time: 10 minutes Serves: 2 Cook time: 10 minutes)*

- 1 tablespoon unsalted butter
- 2 cloves garlic, sliced
- ¼ cup dry white wine
- Kosher salt to taste
- freshly ground pepper to taste
- lemon wedges to serve

- 1 tablespoon extra-virgin olive oil
- zest of ½ lemon
- Juice of ½ lemon
- ¾ pound large tail-on shrimp, peeled
- 1 ½ pounds zucchini, trimmed
- ¼ cup chopped fresh parsley

Preparation Method:

1. Make zucchini noodles of the zucchini using a spiralizer or julienne peeler.
2. Add butter and oil into a skillet and place it over medium heat. When butter melts, add garlic and cook for about a minute until you get a pleasant aroma.
3. Stir in wine, lemon juice, and lemon zest. Cook until dry. Stir in shrimp and cook for about 3 minutes or until just tender. Stir in salt and pepper and remove shrimp into a bowl.
4. Add zucchini noodles to the pan. Add salt and pepper to taste and toss well. Cook for about 4 to 5 minutes until tender.
5. Add shrimp back into the pan and toss well. Garnish with parsley and serve with lemon wedges.

Nutrition Per Serve: *Calories: 312 Fat: 15 g Total Carbohydrate: 16 g Net Carbohydrate: 9 g Fiber: 7 g Protein: 28 g (½ the recipe)*

Sour and Sweet Fish

Ingredients: *(Prep Time: 15 minutes Serves: 2 Cook Time: 10 minutes)*

- 1 tablespoon vinegar
- 2 drops stevia
- 1-pound fish chunks
- ¼ cup butter, melted
- Salt and black pepper, to taste

Preparation Method:

1. Put butter and fish chunks in a skillet and cook for about 3 minutes.
2. Add stevia, salt and black pepper and cook for about 10 minutes, stirring continuously.
3. Dish out in a bowl and serve immediately.
4. Place fish in a dish and set aside to cool for meal prepping.
5. Divide it into 2 containers and refrigerate for up to 2 days. Reheat in the microwave before serving.

Nutrition Per Serve: *Calories: 258 Carbs: 2.8g Protein: 24.5g Fat: 16.7g Sugar: 2.7g Sodium: 649mg*

Spinach Chicken

Ingredients: *(Prep Time: 10 minutes Serves: 2 Cook Time: 10 minutes)*

- 2 garlic cloves, minced
- 2 tablespoons unsalted butter, divided
- ¼ cup parmesan cheese, shredded
- ¾ pound chicken tenders
- ¼ cup heavy cream
- 10 ounces frozen spinach, chopped
- Salt and black pepper, to taste

Preparation Method:

1. Heat 1 tablespoon of butter in a large skillet and add chicken, salt, and black pepper.
2. Cook for about 3 minutes on both sides and remove the chicken to a bowl. Melt remaining butter in the skillet and add garlic, cheese, heavy cream, and spinach.
3. Cook for about 2 minutes and add the chicken. Cook for about 5 minutes on low heat and dish out to immediately serve.
4. Place chicken in a dish and set aside to cool for meal prepping. Divide it into 2 containers and cover them.
5. Refrigerate for about 3 days and reheat in microwave before serving.

Nutrition Per Serve: Calories: 288 Carbs: 3.6g Protein: 27.7g Fat: 18.3g Sugar: 0.3g

White Fish with Lemon

Ingredients: *(Prep Time: 8 minutes Serves: 2 Cook Time: 25 minutes)*

- oz. each (2 cod/hake/tilapia/haddock) fillets,1-inch thickness

For the Rub:

- ½ tsp. garlic powder
- ½ tsp. onion powder
- 1 Tbsp. fresh lemon juice
- kosher salt
- olive oil

For Garnish:

- ½ red/yellow/white onion, cut into strips
- 1 small bell pepper, wedges
- lettuce
- 4 cherry tomatoes
- 2 Tbsp. olive oil
- salt and pepper to taste

Preparation Method:

1. Thoroughly combine all rub ingredients. Lightly drizzle the fish fillets with olive oil. Rub the fish with the garlic-onion mixture.
2. You can grill, roast, or fry the fish, according to your preference.
3. heat olive oil in a frying pan. Cook for 3–5 minutes on each side. OR preheat your oven to 400°F (205°C) and bake the fish for 15–20 minutes.
4. Toss vegetables with olive oil, salt, and pepper.
5. Serve the fish with the vegetable salad drizzled with lime juice.

Nutrition Per Serving: *Calories: 178, Net Carbs: 7.5 g, Total Fat: 1.8 g, Cholesterol 83 mg, Sodium 112 mg, Total Carbohydrate: 9.4 g, Fiber: 1.9 g, Total Sugars 5.5 g, Protein: 31.5 g*

Tuna Fishcakes

Ingredients: *(Prep Time: 10 minutes Serves: 5 cutlets Cook Time: 10 minutes)*

- 2 5 oz. cans tuna, drained and shredded
- 1 garlic clove, crushed
- ½ cup Parmesan, grated
- 1 cup keto breadcrumbs
- ¼ cup feta cheese/Mozzarella, crumbled
- 2 whole eggs, slightly beaten
- ½ lemon, juice and zest

- 2 Tbsp. Greek yogurt
- 2 Tbsp. olive oil
- 2 Tbsp. Dijon mustard
- 1 tsp. herbs de Provence/smoked paprika/thyme
- kosher salt and black pepper
- 2 Tbsp. fresh dill, chopped

Preparation Method:

1. Combine all the ingredients in a large bowl and mix well.
2. Shape the tuna mixture into 5 patties using your hands.
3. You can grill them or fry them in a skillet. Cook for 5 minutes on each side until golden brown.
4. Serve warm with grilled or fresh vegetables.

Nutritional Per Serve: *Calories: 230, Net Carbs: 8.4 g, Total Fat: 12.4 g, Cholesterol 88 mg, Sodium 437 mg, Total Carbohydrate: 11.4 g, Fiber: 3 g, Total Sugars .9 g, Protein: 20.3 g*

Zucchini Pizza

Ingredients: *(Prep Time: 10 minutes Serves: 2 Cook Time: 15 minutes)*

- 1/8 cup spaghetti sauce
- ½ zucchini, cut in circular slices
- ½ cup cream cheese
- Pepperoni slices, for topping
- ½ cup mozzarella cheese, shredded

Preparation Method:

1. Preheat the oven to 350 degrees and grease a baking dish. Arrange the zucchini on the baking dish and layer with spaghetti sauce.
2. Top with pepperoni slices and mozzarella cheese.
3. Transfer the baking dish to the oven and bake for about 15 minutes.
4. Remove from the oven and serve immediately.

Nutrition Per Serve: *Calories: 445 Carbs: 3.6g Protein: 12.8g Fat: 42g Sugar: 0.3g Sodium: 429mg*

Dinner Recipes

Authentic Turkey Kebabs

Ingredients: *(Prep Time: 15 minutes Servings: 6 Cooking Time: 30 minutes)*

- 1 ½ pounds turkey breast, cubed
- 3 Spanish peppers, sliced
- 2 zucchinis, cut into thick slices
- 1 onion, cut into wedges
- 2 tablespoons olive oil, room temperature
- 1 tablespoon dry ranch seasoning

Preparation Method:

1. Thread the turkey pieces and vegetables onto bamboo skewers. Sprinkle the skewers with dry ranch seasoning and olive oil.
2. Grill your kebabs for about 10 minutes, turning them periodically to ensure even cooking.
3. Wrap your kebabs in foil before packing them into airtight containers; keep them in your refrigerator for up to 3 days.

Nutrition Per Serve: *Calories: 2 Fat: 13.8g Carbs: 6.7g Protein: 25.8g Fiber: 1.2g*

Brie-Stuffed Meatballs

Ingredients: *(Prep Time: 15 minutes Cook Time: 25 minutes Serves: 5)*

- 2 eggs, beaten
- 1-pound ground pork
- 1/3 cup double cream
- 1 tablespoon fresh parsley
- Kosher salt and ground black pepper
- 1 teaspoon dried rosemary
- 10 (1-inch cubes) of brie cheese
- 2 tablespoons scallions, minced
- 2 cloves garlic, minced

Preparation Method:

1. Mix all ingredients, except for the brie cheese, until everything is well incorporated.
2. Roll the mixture into 10 patties.
3. Place cheese in the center of each patty and roll into a ball—roast in the preheated oven at 0 degrees F for about 20 minutes.

Nutrition Per Serve: *Calories: 302 Fat: 13g Carbs: 1.9g Protein: 33.4g Fiber: 0.3g*

Chicken Stew with Vegetables

Ingredients: *(Prep Time: 10 minutes Serves: 4 Cook Time: 30 minutes)*

- 1 lb. chicken fillets, chopped
- 1 can (14 oz.) artichoke hearts, drained
- 4 ripe tomatoes, chopped
- 1 white onion (70 g), diced
- 2 garlic cloves, minced
- 1 red bell pepper, chopped
- 3 tbsp. herbs de Provence
- Sea salt and black pepper

Preparation Method:

1. Heat a cast-iron skillet over medium heat. Add chicken fillets, and cook for 10–15 minutes until lightly browned.
2. Add garlic and onion and sauté for 5 minutes, stirring often.
3. Add herbs de Provence, artichoke hearts, chopped bell peppers, and tomatoes, and cook for 8–10 minutes over medium-high heat.
4. Remove from heat and serve.

Nutrition Per Serve: *Calories: 307, Net Carbs: 12.6 g, Total Carbohydrates: 20.5 g, Total Fat: 8.9 g, Cholesterol 101 mg, Sodium 199 mg, Protein: 37.4 g, Fiber: 7.9 g, Sugar: 6.9 g*

Coconut Shrimp Skillet

Ingredients: *(Prep Time: 15 minutes Serves: 2 Cook Time: 15 minutes)*

- 2 tablespoons extra-virgin avocado oil, divided
- 2 mediums (31.1 oz.) spring onions, parts separated and chopped
- 3 cloves garlic, minced
- 1 medium (0.5 oz.) red chile pepper, chopped
- 8.8 ounces raw peeled shrimp
- ¼ cup (2.2 oz.) coconut butter
- Salt and black pepper, to taste
- 2 tablespoons extra-virgin olive oil
- 2 mediums (14.1 oz.) zucchini, spiralized

Preparation Method:

1. Heat a skillet greased with 1 tablespoon of the avocado oil over medium-high heat. Add the white parts of the spring onions, garlic, and chile pepper. Cook for 1 to 2 minutes, until fragrant.
2. Add the shrimp and cook for about 2 minutes, until opaque. Add the coconut butter, stir to combine, and season with salt and pepper. Remove from the heat and set aside.
3. Use a spatula to transfer the entire contents of the pan to a bowl. Drizzle with the olive oil and season to taste. Sprinkle with the reserved spring onions.
4. Grease the pan with the remaining 1 tablespoon avocado oil. Add the "zoodles" and cook for 1 to 3 minutes, tossing to ensure even cooking. Top with the cooked shrimp, then remove from the heat.
5. Serve warm or let cool and store in the fridge in a sealed container for up to 3 days.

Nutrition Per Serve: *Calories: 555 kcal Total carbs: 16.8 g Fiber: 7.4 g Net Carbs: 9.4 g Protein: 23.1 g Fat: 46.8 g*

Creamy Chicken Stew

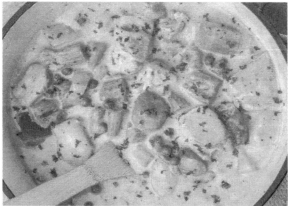

Ingredients: *(Prep Time: 8 minutes Servings: 4 Cook Time: 30 minutes)*

- 4chicken breasts
- 4Tbsp. salted butter
- 4oz. sun-dried tomatoes, diced
- oz. fresh spinach, chopped
- 4oz. parmesan, grated

- 1 cup heavy cream
- 2 garlic cloves, crushed
- kosher salt and ground black pepper
- Olive oil

Preparation Method:

1 Preheat olive oil in the frying pan. Season chicken breasts with salt and pepper.
2 Fry them in the pan for 10 minutes or until golden brown, flipping halfway through.
3 Melt the butter in a skillet. Add chopped sun-dried tomatoes and crushed garlic and sauté for 5–7 minutes.
4 Add spinach and continue to cook, stirring occasionally. Add heavy cream and shredded Parmesan.

5   Submerge the cooked chicken breasts in the sauce and let them simmer gently for 10 minutes.

6   Serve with fresh salad, grilled vegetables, or crusty keto bread.

Nutrition Per Serve: *Calories: 682, Net Carbs: 4.3 g, Total Carbohydrates: 5.3 g, Total Fat: 52.4 g, Cholesterol 249 mg, Sodium 474 mg, Protein: 48.4 g, Fiber: 1 g, Sugar: 0.9 g*

Flatbread with Chicken Liver Pâté

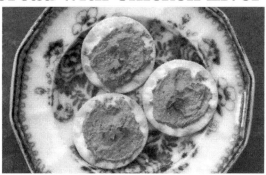

Ingredients: *(Prep Time: 15 minutes Cook Time: 2 hours 15 minutes Serves: 4)*

- 1 yellow onion, finely chopped
- 10 ounces' chicken livers
- 1/2 teaspoon Mediterranean seasoning blend
- 4 tablespoons olive oil
- 1 garlic clove, minced

- For Flatbread:
- 1 cup lukewarm water
- 1/2 stick butter
- 1/2 cup flax meal
- 1 ½ tablespoons psyllium husks
- 1 ¼ cups almond flour

Preparation Method:

1   Pulse the chicken livers along with the seasoning blend, olive oil, onion, and garlic in your food processor; reserve.

2   Mix the dry ingredients for the flatbread.

3   Mix in all the wet ingredients. Whisk to combine well.

4   Set aside at room temperature within 2 hours. Split the dough into 8 balls and roll them out on a flat surface.

5   In a lightly greased pan, cook your flatbread for 1 minute on each side or until golden.

Nutrition Per Serve: *Calories: 395 Fat: 30.2g Carbs: 3.6g Protein: 17.9g Fiber: 0.5g*

Golden Scallops

Ingredients: *(Prep Time: 7 minutes Serves: 4 Cook Time: 5 minutes)*

- 1 lb. sea scallops
- 2 garlic cloves, minced
- 1 Tbsp. lemon juice
- 2 Tbsp. fresh oregano, chopped

- 2 Tbsp. avocado oil/salted butter, melted
- kosher salt, and pepper
- Red pepper flakes

Preparation Method:

1. Season scallops with salt and pepper.
2. Heat avocado oil/salted butter in a cast iron skillet or frying pan. Add minced garlic.
3. Arrange scallops in a single layer in the skillet. Cook for 2–3 minutes, depending on the size of the scallops, flipping them once during the cooking process.
4. Add lemon juice, red pepper flakes, chopped oregano, olive oil, salt, and pepper to a small bowl and whisk to combine.
5. Serve scallops with lemon dressing on a bed of mashed broccoli.

Nutrition Per Serve: *Calories: 118, Net Carbs: 3.8 g, Total Fat: 2 g, Cholesterol: 37 mg, Sodium: 183 mg, Total Carbohydrate: 5.1 g, Fiber: 1.3 g, Total Sugars: 0.2 g, Protein: 19.3 g*

Grilled Lamb Chops

Ingredients: *(Prep Time: 4 hours & 15 minutes Cook Time: 15 minutes Serves: 4)*

- 8-3 ounces' lamb loin chops

Marinade:

- 1 small sliced onion
- 2 tablespoons of red wine vinegar
- 1 tablespoon of lemon juice
- 1 tablespoon of olive oil
- 2 teaspoons fresh minced rosemary

- 2 teaspoons of Dijon mustard
- 1 minced garlic clove
- 1/2 teaspoon pepper
- 1/4 teaspoon salt
- 1/4 teaspoon of ground ginger

Preparation Method:

1. Coat the lamb chops with the combined marinade mixture.
2. Cover and refrigerate for 4 hours or overnight.
3. Drain and discard marinade.
4. Lightly oil your grill rack. Grill lamb chops for 4 to 7 minutes on each side over medium heat. Serve.

Nutrition Per Serve: *Calories: 164 Carbohydrates: 0g Fiber: 0g Fats: 8g Sodium: 112 mg Protein: 21g*

Lamb Chops Curry

Ingredients: *(Prep Time: 15 minutes Cook Time: 30 minutes Serves: 2)*

- 4-4 ounces' bone-in loin chops of lamb
- 1 tablespoon of canola oil
- 3/4 cup of orange juice
- 2 tablespoons teriyaki sauce reduced-sodium
- 2 teaspoons of grated orange zest
- 1 teaspoon of curry powder
- 1garlic clove, minced
- 1 teaspoon corn-starch
- 2 tablespoons of cold water

Preparation Method:

1   Brown lamb chops on both sides over canola oil. Combine the other five ingredients and pour them over the skillet.
2   Cover and let it simmer for 15 to 20 minutes or until lamb turns tender. Remove from heat and keep warm.
3   Combine the last two ingredients until smooth. Mix into the pan drippings and boil for 2 minutes or until it thickens.
4   Serve with steamed rice if desired.

Nutrition Per Serve: *Calories: 337 Carbohydrates: 15g Fiber: 1g Fats: 17g Sodium: 402 mg Protein: 30g*

Old-Fashioned Goulash

Ingredients: *(Prep Time: 15 minutes Serves: 4 Cook Time: 9 hours 10 minutes)*

- 1 ½ pound pork butt, chopped
- 1 teaspoon sweet Hungarian paprika
- 2 Hungarian hot peppers, deveined and minced
- 1 cup leeks, chopped
- 1 ½ tablespoons lard
- 1 teaspoon caraway seeds, ground
- 4 cups vegetable broth
- 2 garlic cloves, crushed
- 1 teaspoon cayenne pepper
- 2 cups tomato sauce with herbs

- 1 ½ pound pork butt, chopped
- 1 teaspoon sweet Hungarian paprika
- 2 Hungarian hot peppers, deveined and minced
- 1 cup leeks, chopped
- 1 ½ tablespoons lard
- 1 teaspoon caraway seeds, ground
- 4 cups vegetable broth
- 2 garlic cloves, crushed
- 1 teaspoon cayenne pepper
- 2 cups tomato sauce with herbs

Preparation Method:

1. Melt the lard in a heavy-bottomed pot over medium-high heat. Sear the pork for 5 to 6 minutes until just browned on all sides; set aside.
2. Add in the leeks and garlic; continue to cook until they have softened.
3. Place the reserved pork along with the sautéed mixture in your crockpot. Put in the other fixings and stir to combine.
4. Cover with the lid and slow cook for 9 hours on the lowest setting.

Nutrition Per Serve: *Calories: 456 Fat: 27g Carbs: 6.7g Protein: 32g Fiber: 3.4g*

Parmesan-Crusted Pork

Ingredients: *(Prep Time: 8 minutes Serves: 4 Cook Time: 20 minutes)*

- 4pork chops (5 oz. each, 1-inch thick), boneless
- ½ cup parmesan/cheddar cheese, grated
- 2 garlic cloves, minced

- 2 Tbsp. olive oil
- ¼ tsp. kosher salt
- 1 tsp. onion powder
- 1 tsp. paprika
- ¼ tsp. ground black pepper

Preparation Method:

1 Brush pork chops with olive oil. Mix grated cheese with spices, minced garlic, and salt. Cover the pork chops with the cheese mixture.

2 Preheat your oven to 400°F (205°C). Heat olive oil in a skillet. Cook the pork chops for 2 minutes on each side.

3 Transfer them to a baking pan and bake for 13–18 minutes, flipping the pork halfway through. Serve with lemon or lime wedges.

Nutrition Per Serve: *Calories: 562, Net Carbs: 1.6 g, Total Carbohydrates: 1.9 g, Total Fat: 45.1 g, Cholesterol 131 mg, Sodium 238 mg, Protein: 36.8 g, Fiber: 0.3 g, Sugar: 0.3 g*

Pork Cutlets in Cucumber Sauce

Ingredients: *(Prep Time: 4 hours & 15 minutes Serves: 4 Cook Time: 15 minutes)*

Marinade:

- 16 ounces' pork tenderloin, cut into ½-inch thick slices
- 1 small chopped onion
- 2 tablespoons of lemon juice
- 1 tablespoon fresh minced parsley
- 2 minced garlic cloves
- 3/4 teaspoon of dried thyme
- 1/8 teaspoon pepper

Cucumber Sauce:

- 1 small seeded and chopped tomato
- 2/3 cup plain yogurt, reduced-fat
- 1/2 cup seeded cucumber, chopped
- 1 tablespoon onion, finely chopped
- 1/2 teaspoon of lemon juice
- 1/8 teaspoon of garlic powder

Preparation Method:

1. Mix all the marinade fixings and marinate the chops for 4 hours (or overnight).
2. Cover and refrigerate. Combine all the cucumber sauce ingredients and mix. Cover and refrigerate.
3. Drain and discard marinade—place chops on a greased broiler pan.
4. Broil for 6 to 8 minutes, each side 4-inch from the heat. Serve with cucumber sauce.

Nutrition Per Serve: *Calories: 177 Carbohydrates: 8g Fiber: 1g Fats: 5g Sodium: 77 mg*

Pork Tenderloin

Ingredients: *(Prep time: 5 minutes; Serves: 6 Cook Time: 15 minutes)*

- 1-pound pastured pork tenderloin, halved
- 1 ½ teaspoon salt
- ¾ teaspoon cracked black pepper
- 1 tablespoon olive oil

Preparation Method:

1 Place a large frying pan over medium heat, add oil and when hot, add pork tenderloin.
2 Cook for 5 to 7 minutes per side until nicely browned and cooked through.
3 When done, transfer pork tenderloin onto a cutting board, let sit for 5 minutes and then slice into 1-inch pieces.
4 Serve straightaway.

Nutrition Per Serve: *Calories: 330 Cal, Carbs: 0 g, Fat: 15 g, Protein: 47 g, Fiber: 0 g.*

Pork Spare Ribs

Ingredients: *(Prep Time: 5 minutes; Serves: 2 Cooking Time: 3 hours)*

- 2 racks of pork ribs, pastured
- 1 tablespoon sea salt
- 1/2 teaspoon cracked black pepper
- 1/2 teaspoon red chili powder
- 1 tablespoon coriander
- 1/2 teaspoon cumin
- 1/2 teaspoon cinnamon
- 2 tablespoons cocoa powder, unsweetened

Preparation Method:

1 Set oven to 350 degrees F and let preheat.
2 In the meantime, whisk together all the ingredients except for pork in a bowl and then rub this mixture on pork ribs until well coated.
3 Then cover ribs with aluminum foil and bake for 3 hours or until cooked through.
4 Serve straightaway.

Nutrition Per Serve: *Calories: 26 Cal, Carbs: 1 g, Fat: 2 g, Protein: 0 g, Fiber: 0 g.*

Roasted Leg Lamb

Ingredients: *(Prep Time: 15 minutes Serves: 12 Cook Time: 2 hours & 30 minutes)*

- 1-112 to 144 ounces' bone-in lamb leg, trimmed

- 1 cup of chicken broth

Marinade:

- 1/3 cup fresh minced rosemary
- 2 tablespoons of Dijon mustard
- 2 tablespoons of olive oil
- 8minced garlic cloves

- 1 teaspoon soy sauce reduced-sodium
- 1/2 teaspoon salt
- 1/2 teaspoon pepper

Preparation Method:

1 Preheat your oven to 325°F. Combine marinade ingredients and coat the lamb. Refrigerate with cover overnight.
2 Place the lamb on a rack using a shallow roasting pan with the fat side up.
3 Bake without cover for 1 ½ hour. Pour the broth, then cover loosely using foil. Bake for another 1 ½ hours or until meat turns to your desired doneness.
4 Let the lamb cool for 10 to 15 minutes before slicing.

Nutrition Per Serve: *Calories: 246 Carbohydrates: 2g Fiber: 0g Fats: 11g Sodium: 320 mg Protein: 33g*

White Fish Casserole

Ingredients: *(Prep Time: 15 minutes Serves: 4 Cook Time: 20 minutes)*

- 1½ lb. white fish fillet (halibut or cod)
- kosher salt, black pepper, olive oil
- 1 lemon
- 1 bell pepper, chopped
- 8 oz. (230 g) halved cherry tomatoes
- 3 oz. (85 g) olives, sliced
- 1 cup (225 g) mozzarella, shredded
- 3 Tbsp. red onion, diced
- 5 garlic cloves, minced
- 2 Tbsp. herbs de Provence

Preparation Method:

1. Preheat your oven to 425°F (220°C). Brush a baking dish with olive oil. Pat the fish dry with a paper towel. Season all over with salt and pepper.
2. Arrange the fish in the baking dish and sprinkle with the juice of half a lemon. Combine olives, tomatoes, bell peppers, onions, garlic, a pinch of salt and pepper, 3 tablespoons of olive oil, and spices in a bowl and mix well.
3. Pour tomato mixture over the fish. Sprinkle with shredded cheese.
4. Bake for 15–20 minutes. At the 15-minute mark, check if the fish is done by inserting a fork and twisting. If the fish flakes easily, it is done.
5. Remove from the oven and serve.

Nutrition Per Serve: *Calories: 297, Net Carbs: 7 g, Total Carbohydrates: 9.3 g, Protein: 39.5 g, Fat: 11.3 g, Fiber: 2.3 g, Cholesterol 59 mg, Sodium 323 mg, Total Sugars 3.7 g*

Sirloin Beef Roast

Ingredients: *(Prep Time: 10 minutes; Serves: 6 Cook Time: 1 hour and 30 minutes)*

- 2-pound beef roast, grass-fed
- 2 medium zucchini, cut into 1-inch chunks
- 2 medium butternut squash, cut into 1-inch chunks
- 1/2 cup cherry tomato, halved
- 1 teaspoon salt, divided
- 1/8 teaspoon cracked black pepper
- 1 teaspoon dried basil, divided
- 1/2 teaspoon dried oregano
- 1 tablespoon lemon juice
- 3tablespoons olive oil, divided

Preparation Method:

1. Set oven to 325 degrees F and let preheat. Whisk together ½ teaspoon salt, black pepper, ½ teaspoon basil, oregano, and 1 tablespoon oil until well mixed and then rub this mixture all over beef roast. Place the beef in a roasting pan and bake for 45 minutes.
2. Meanwhile, whisk together remaining salt and basil, lemon juice and remaining olive oil in a large bowl.
3. Add zucchini, squash, and tomato and toss until well coated.
4. After 45 minutes of roasting, place seasoned vegetables around the beef and continue roasting for another 45 minutes until beef is medium done.
5. When done, slice roast and serve with vegetables.

Nutrition Per Serve: *Calories: 248 Cal, Carbs: 1.5 g, Fat: 5.7 g, Protein: 44.2 g, Fiber: 0.3 g.*

Spicy Chicken Breasts

Ingredients: *(Prep Time: 15 minutes Serves: 6 Cook Time: 30 minutes)*

- 1 ½ pounds chicken breasts
- 1 bell pepper, deveined and chopped
- 1 leek, chopped
- 1 tomato, pureed
- 2 tablespoons coriander
- 2 garlic cloves, minced

- 1 teaspoon cayenne pepper
- 1 teaspoon dry thyme
- 1/4 cup coconut amino
- Sea salt
- Ground black pepper

Preparation Method:

1. Rub each chicken breasts with garlic, cayenne pepper, thyme, salt, and black pepper.
2. Cook the chicken in a saucepan over medium-high heat.
3. Sear for about 5 minutes until golden brown on all sides.
4. Fold in the tomato puree and coconut amino and bring it to a boil. Add in the pepper, leek, and coriander.
5. Reduce the heat to simmer. Continue to cook, partially covered, for about 20 minutes.

Nutrition Per Serve: *Calories: 239 Fat: 6g Carbs: 5.5g Protein: 34.3g Fiber: 1g*

Sunday Chicken with Cauliflower Salad

Ingredients: *(Prep Time: 15 minutes Serves: 2Cook Time: 20 minutes)*

- 1 teaspoon hot paprika
- 2 tablespoons fresh basil, snipped
- 1/2 cup mayonnaise
- 1 teaspoon mustard
- 2 teaspoons butter
- 2 chicken wings

- 1/2 cup cheddar cheese, shredded
- Sea salt
- Ground black pepper
- 2 tablespoons dry sherry
- 1 shallot, finely minced
- 1/2 head of cauliflower

Preparation Method:

1. Boil the cauliflower with salted water in a pot until it has softened; cut into small florets and place in a salad bowl.
2. Melt the butter in a saucepan over medium-high heat. Cook the chicken for about 8 minutes or until the skin is crisp and browned.
3. Season with hot paprika salt, and black pepper.
4. Whisk the mayonnaise, mustard, dry sherry, and shallot, and dress your salad.
5. Top with cheddar cheese and fresh basil.

Nutrition Per Serve: *Calories: 444 Fat: 36g Carbs: 5.7g Protein: 20.6g Fiber: 4.3g*

Turkey Chorizo with Bok Choy

Ingredients: *(Prep Time: 15 minutes Serves: 4 Cook Time: 50 minutes)*

- 4 mild turkey Chorizo, sliced
- 1/2 cup full-fat milk
- 6 ounces Gruyere cheese, preferably freshly grated
- 1 yellow onion, chopped
- Coarse salt
- Ground black pepper
- 1-pound Bok choy, tough stem ends trimmed
- 1 cup cream of mushroom soup
- 1 tablespoon lard, room temperature

Preparation Method:

1. Melt the lard in a non-stick skillet over a moderate flame; cook the Chorizo sausage for about 5 minutes, occasionally stirring to ensure even cooking; reserve.
2. Add in the onion, salt, pepper, Bok choy, and cream of mushroom soup. Continue to cook for 4 minutes longer or until the vegetables have softened.
3. Put the batter into a lightly oiled casserole dish. Top with the reserved Chorizo. In a mixing bowl, thoroughly combine the milk and cheese.
4. Pour the cheese mixture over the sausage. Cover with foil and bake at 36degrees F for about 35 minutes.

Nutrition Per Serve: Calories: 18 Fat: 12g Carbs: 2.6g Protein: 9.4g Fiber: 1g

Snacks and Appetizer Recipes

Artichoke and Spinach Dip

Ingredients: (Prep time: 10 minutes Serves: 4 Cook time: 20 minutes)

- 8 ounces' cream cheese, softened
- 1/2 cup mayonnaise
- 1/4 cup grated Parmesan cheese
- 1/4 cup grated mozzarella cheese
- 1 clove garlic, minced
- 1/2 teaspoon dried basil
- 1/2 teaspoon dried oregano
- 1/2 teaspoon dried thyme
- 1/2 cup chopped frozen spinach
- 1/2 cup chopped canned artichoke hearts, drained
- Salt and pepper to taste

Preparation Method:

1. Preheat the oven to 350°F (175°C).
2. In a mixing bowl, combine the softened cream cheese, mayonnaise, Parmesan cheese, mozzarella cheese, minced garlic, dried basil, dried oregano, and dried thyme. Mix well.
3. Add the chopped spinach and artichoke hearts to the mixture. Stir until well combined.
4. Season with salt and pepper to taste. Transfer the mixture to an oven-safe dish and smooth the top.
5. Bake in the preheated oven for 20 minutes, or until the top is golden and bubbly. Remove from the oven and let it cool for a few minutes before serving.

Nutrition Per Serve: *Calories: 270 Protein: 7g Carbohydrates: 5g Fat: 25g Fiber: 2g Cholesterol: 60mg Sodium: 480mg Potassium: 150mg*

Burrata Caprese Stack

Ingredients: (Prep Time: 5 minutes Serves 4)

- 1 large organic tomato, preferably heirloom
- ½ teaspoon salt
- ¼ teaspoon freshly ground black pepper
- 1 (4-ounce) ball burrata cheese
- 8 fresh basil leaves, thinly sliced
- 2 tablespoons extra-virgin olive oil
- 1 tablespoon red wine or balsamic vinegar

Preparation Method:

1. Slice the tomato into 4 thick slices, removing any tough center core and sprinkle with salt and pepper. Place the tomatoes, seasoned-side up, on a plate.
2. On a separate rimmed plate, slice the burrata into 4 thick slices and place one slice on top of each tomato slice.
3. Top each with one-quarter of the basil and pour any reserved burrata cream from the rimmed plate over top. Drizzle with olive oil and vinegar and serve with a fork and knife.

Nutrition Per Serve: *Calories: 153, Total Fat: 13g, Total Carbs: 2g, Net Carbs: 1g, Fiber: 1g, Protein: 7g; Sodium: 469mg (1 stack).*

Cauliflower Falafel

Ingredients: *(Prep Time: 10 minutes Serves: 16 Cook Time: 20 minutes)*

- 1 Tbsp. avocado oil
- 1 cup celery stalks, chopped
- 1 Tbsp. chia seeds
- ½ tsp. ground paprika
- ¼ cup coconut flour/almond flour
- 1 tsp. ground cumin
- 1 Tbsp. onion flakes
- ½ cup cilantro leaves, finely chopped
- 4 garlic cloves, minced
- 2 cups cauliflower rice
- Sea salt
- 2½ Tbsp. water

Preparation Method:

1. Preheat the oven to 350°F (180°C). Mix the cauliflower, celery, coconut flour, minced garlic, paprika, dried onion, avocado oil, and salt in a large bowl.
2. Add chia seeds and water and stir until the mixture achieves a dough-like consistency.
3. Pull off a walnut-sized piece of dough and roll it into a ball between greased palms.
4. Place the falafel balls on a greased baking sheet.
5. Bake the falafels for 15–20 minutes until lightly brown.

Nutrition Per Serve: *Calories: 20, Net Carbs: 1.5 g, Total Carbohydrates: 3.1 g, Total Fat: 0.9 g, Cholesterol 0 mg, Sodium 11 mg, Protein: 0.7 g, Fiber: 1.6 g, Sugar: 0.6 g*

Citrus-Marinated Olives

Ingredients: *(Prep Time: 10 minutes Serves: 2 cups)*

- 2 cups mixed green olives with pits
- ¼ cup red wine vinegar
- ¼ cup extra-virgin olive oil
- 4 garlic cloves, finely minced
- Zest and juice of
- 2 clementines or 1 large orange
- 1 teaspoon red pepper flakes
- 2 bay leaves
- ½ teaspoon ground cumin
- ½ teaspoon ground allspice

Preparation Method:

1. In a large glass bowl or jar, combine the olives, vinegar, oil, garlic, orange zest and juice, red pepper flakes, bay leaves, cumin, and allspice and mix well.
2. Cover and refrigerate for at least 4 hours or up to a week to allow the olives to marinate, tossing again before serving.

Nutrition Per Serve: *Calories: 133, Total Fat: 14g, Total Carbs: 3g, Net Carbs: 1g, Fiber: 2g, Protein: 1g; Sodium: 501mg (¼ cup)*

Classic Stuffed Mushrooms

Ingredients: *(Prep Time: 10 minutes Serves: 16 Cook Time: 25 minutes)*

- 16 (1 lb.) fresh button mushrooms, rinsed and dried
- 2 shallots, chopped
- ½ cup keto breadcrumbs
- 2 Tbsp. walnuts, chopped
- 1 minced garlic clove
- ½ tsp. garlic powder
- 2 Tbsp. unsalted butter/cream cheese
- 4 oz. parmesan, shredded
- ½ tsp. dried Italian herbs
- 1 Tbsp. olive oil

Preparation Method:

1. Remove the stems from the mushrooms and scoop out the centers. Chop them finely.
2. Mix the chopped stems with the remaining ingredients (except the olive oil) for the filling.
3. Fill the mushroom caps with the stuffing. Preheat your oven to 400°F (205°C). Line a baking dish with parchment paper and grease with olive oil.
4. Arrange mushrooms in a single layer in the baking dish. Sprinkle the shredded cheese and olive oil over the mushrooms.
5. Bake for 25 minutes. Your perfect Mediterranean appetizer is ready.

Nutrition Per Serve: *Calories: 57, Net Carbs: 1.5 g, Total Carbs: 1.9 g, Total Fat: 4.5 g, Chol: 9 mg, Sodium 85 mg, Protein: 3.4 g, Fiber: 0.4 g, Sugar: 0.4 g*

Flavored Roasted Seed and Nut Mix

Ingredients: (Prep Time: 4 minutes Serves: 1 cup Cook Time: 12 minutes)

- 1 cup raw keto nut mix (almonds, pecans, walnuts, hazelnuts)
- Seeds (sunflower, pumpkin, etc.)

- 1 tsp. coconut oil/olive oil/butter, melted

optional

For sweet nut mix

- granulated sweetener
- cinnamon

- pumpkin pie spice

For spicy nut mix

- herbs
- nutmeg

- smoked paprika/curry
- onion/garlic/chili powder

Preparation Method:

1. Preheat your oven to 350°F (180°C).
2. In a small bowl, combine nuts and seeds with your favorite seasoning. Ensure you coat them well.
3. Line a baking sheet with parchment paper.
4. Arrange the nut-seed mixture in a single layer on the baking sheet and bake for 8–12 minutes until fragrant. Stir twice during this time.
5. Serve warm or cold. You can eat them alone as a snack, but they are perfect in soups, salads, meat meals, or even desserts.

Nutrition Per Serve: *Calories: 798, Net Carbs: 9.3 g, Total Carbs: 26.9 g, Total Fat: 69.8 g, Chol: 0 mg, Sodium 1 mg, Protein: 27.9 g, Fiber: 17.6 g, Sugar: 5.7 g*

Goat Cheese–Mackerel Pâté

Ingredients: *(Prep Time: 10 minutes Serves 4)*

- 4 ounces' olive oil-packed wild-caught mackerel
- 2 ounces' goat cheese
- Zest and juice of 1 lemon
- 2 tablespoons chopped fresh parsley

- 2 tablespoons chopped fresh arugula
- 1 tablespoon extra-virgin olive oil
- 2 teaspoons chopped capers
- 1 to 2 teaspoons fresh horseradish (optional)

For Serving (Optional)

Crackers

- cucumber rounds
- endive spears

- celery

Preparation Method:

1. In a food processor, blender, or large bowl with immersion blender, combine the mackerel, goat cheese, lemon zest and juice, parsley, arugula, olive oil, capers, and horseradish (if using). Process or blend until smooth and creamy.
2. Serve with crackers, cucumber rounds, endive spears, or celery. 3.Store covered in the refrigerator for up to 1 week.

Nutrition Per Serve: *Calories: 118, Total Fat: 8g, Total Carbs: 1g, Net Carbs: 1g, Fiber: 0g, Protein: 9g; Sodium: 196mg*

Grilled Portobello Mushrooms

Ingredients: *(Prep Time: 10 minutes Servings: 4 Cook Time: 10 minutes)*

- 3 Tbsp. balsamic vinegar
- ½ tsp. onion powder
- 2 Tbsp. avocado oil
- 4 large Portobello mushrooms
- 1 - 2 tsp. liquid smoke

- 1 garlic clove, minced
- kosher salt, ground pepper
- 3 Tbsp. soy sauce
- 1 Tbsp. Worcestershire sauce

Preparation Method:

1. Remove the stems from the mushrooms.
2. Combine all ingredients for the marinade (except the mushrooms and oil) in a bowl and mix well.
3. Add the mushrooms to the marinade and let them sit for 20 minutes. Heat a grill or frying pan to medium-high heat.
4. Brush the cooking surface with oil and arrange the mushrooms evenly in one layer. Cook for 5 minutes on each side.
5. You can serve them as an appetizer or assemble them in a sandwich.

Nutrition Per Serve: *Calories: 49, Net Carbs: 4.8 g, Total Carbohydrates: 6.4 g, Total Fat: 0.7 g, Cholesterol 0 mg, Sodium 719 mg, Protein: 4.7 g, Fiber: 1.6 g, Sugar: 1.1 g*

Greek Deviled Eggs

Ingredients: *(Prep Time: 15 minutes Serves 4 Cook Time: 15 minutes)*

- 4 large hardboiled eggs
- 2 tablespoons Roasted Garlic Aioli
- ½ cup finely crumbled feta cheese
- 8 pitted Kalamata olives, finely chopped
- 2 tablespoons chopped sun-dried tomatoes

- 1 tablespoon minced red onion
- ½ teaspoon dried dill
- ¼ teaspoon freshly ground black pepper

Preparation Method:

1. Slice the hardboiled eggs in half lengthwise, remove the yolks, and place the yolks in a medium bowl. Reserve the egg white halves and set aside.
2. Smash the yolks well with a fork. Add the aioli, feta, olives, sun-dried tomatoes, onion, dill, and pepper and stir to combine until smooth and creamy.
3. Spoon the filling into each egg white half and chill for 30 minutes, or up to 24 hours, covered. Cooking

Nutrition Per Serving: *Calories: 147, Total Fat: 11g, Total Carbs: 3g, Net Carbs: 3g, Fiber: 0g, Protein: 9g; Sodium: 334mg*

Manchego Crackers

Ingredients: *(Serves: 40 crackers Prep Time: 15 minutes Cook Time: 15 minutes)*

- 4 tablespoons butter, at room temperature
- 1 cup finely shredded Manchego cheese
- 1 cup almond flour
- 1 teaspoon salt, divided
- ¼ teaspoon freshly ground black pepper
- 1 large egg

Preparation Method:

1. Using an electric mixer, cream together the butter and shredded cheese until well combined and smooth.
2. In a small bowl, combine the almond flour with ½ teaspoon salt and pepper. Slowly add the almond flour mixture to the cheese, mixing constantly until the dough just comes together to form a ball.
3. Transfer to a piece of parchment or plastic wrap and roll into a cylinder log about 1½ inches thick. Wrap tightly and refrigerate for at least 1 hour.
4. Preheat the oven to 350°F. Line two baking sheets with parchment paper or silicone baking mats.
5. To make the egg wash, in a small bowl, whisk together the egg and remaining ½ teaspoon salt.
6. Slice the refrigerated dough into small rounds, about ¼ inch thick, and place on the lined baking sheets.
7. Brush the tops of the crackers with egg wash and bake until the crackers are golden and crispy, 12 to 15 minutes. Remove from the oven and allow to cool on a wire rack.
8. Serve warm or, once fully cooled, store in an airtight container in the refrigerator for up to 1 week.

Nutrition Per Serving: *Calories: 243, Total Fat: 23g, Total Carbs: 2g, Net Carbs: 1g, Fiber: 1g, Protein: 8g; Sodium: 792mg (10 crackers).*

Mashed Roasted Eggplant with Spice (Ghanoush)

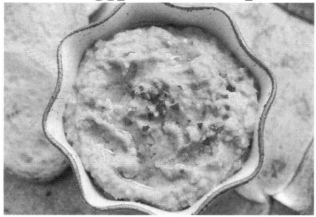

Ingredients: *(Prep Time: 10 minutes Servings: 4 Cook Time: 40 minutes)*

- 1 medium eggplant (1 lb./450 g)
- 1 Tbsp. sesame oil
- 2 Tbsp. tahini
- 2 tsp. lemon juice

- 2 garlic cloves, peeled
- ⅛ tsp. salt
- ⅛ tsp. ground nutmeg
- ½ tsp. paprika/chili

Preparation Method:

1. Preheat your oven to 425°F (220°C). Wrap the garlic cloves in aluminum foil. Poke the eggplant skin with the fork a few times and wrap it in aluminum foil.
2. Roast the garlic in the oven for 15 minutes and the eggplant for 40 minutes. Let the eggplant cool, then peel and chop. Let it drain for 5 minutes.
3. Add the chopped eggplant, roasted garlic cloves, tahini, lemon juice, salt, sesame oil, and nutmeg to the food processor and puree them.
4. Transfer eggplant puree to a serving bowl and garnish with paprika. Serve with keto flatbread, fresh vegetable wedges, or lettuce leaves.

Nutrition Per Serve: *Calories: 111, Net Carbs: 3.8 g, Total Carbs: 8.5 g, Total Fat: 7.6 g, Chol: 0 mg, Sodium 13 mg, Protein: 2.4 g, Fiber: 4.7 g, Sugar: 3.7 g*

Olive Tapenade with Anchovies

Ingredients: (*Prep Time: 10 minutes Serves: 2 cups*)

- 2 cups pitted Kalamata olives
- 2 anchovy fillets, chopped
- 2 teaspoons chopped capers
- 1 garlic clove, finely minced

- 1 cooked egg yolk
- 1 teaspoon Dijon mustard
- ¼ cup extra-virgin olive oil

For serving (optional)

- Seedy Crackers
- Versatile Sandwich Round

- Vegetables

Preparation Method:

1. Rinse the olives in cold water and drain well.
2. In a food processor, blender, or a large jar (if using an immersion blender) place the drained olives, anchovies, capers, garlic, egg yolk, and Dijon. Process until it forms a thick paste.
3. With the food processor running, slowly stream in the olive oil.
4. Transfer to a small bowl, cover, and refrigerate at least 1 hour to let the flavors develop.
5. Serve with Seedy Crackers, atop a Versatile Sandwich Round, or with your favorite crunchy vegetables.

Nutrition Per Serve: *Calories: 179, Total Fat: 19g, Total Carbs: 3g, Net Carbs: 1g, Fiber: 2g, Protein: 2g; Sodium: 812mg (⅓ cup)*

Roasted Vegetable Balls

Ingredients: (Prep Time: 10 minutes Serves: 16 Cook Time: 20 minutes)

- 1 Tbsp. sesame oil
- 1 cup (130 g) celery stalks, chopped
- 1 Tbsp. chia seeds
- ½ tsp. ground paprika
- ¼ cup coconut flour/almond flour
- 1 tsp. ground cumin
- 1 Tbsp. onion flakes
- ½ cup cilantro leaves, finely chopped
- 4 garlic cloves, minced
- 2 cups cauliflower rice
- kosher salt
- 2½ Tbsp. water, at room temperature

Preparation Method:

1. Preheat the oven to 350°F (180°C).
2. Mix all the ingredients together in a large bowl and stir until the mixture achieves a dough-like consistency.
3. Pull off a walnut-sized piece of dough and form a ball between greased palms.
4. Spray a baking sheet with oil. Arrange the falafel balls on it. Bake in the oven for 15–20 minutes until lightly brown.
5. Serve with lettuce leaves and tzatziki sauce.

Nutrition Per Serve: *Calories: 21, Net Carbs: 1.7 g, Total Carbs: 3.2 g, Total Fat: 1 g, Chol: 0 mg, Sodium 12 mg, Protein: 0.8 g, Fiber: 1.5 g, Sugar: 0.5 g*

The Mediterranean Fat Bombs

Ingredients: *(Prep Time: 15 minutes Serves: 6 fat bombs)*

- 1 cup crumbled goat cheese
- 4 tablespoons jarred pesto
- 12 pitted Kalamata olives, finely chopped
- ½ cup finely chopped walnuts
- 1 tablespoon chopped fresh rosemary

Preparation Method:

1. In a medium bowl, combine the goat cheese, pesto, and olives and mix well using a fork. Place in the refrigerator for at least 4 hours to harden.
2. Using your hands, form the mixture into 6 balls, about ¾-inch diameter. The mixture will be sticky.
3. In a small bowl, place the walnuts and rosemary and roll the goat cheese balls in the nut mixture to coat.
4. Store the fat bombs in the refrigerator for up to 1 week or in the freezer for up to 1 month.

Nutrition Per Serving: *Calories: 166, Total Fat: 15g, Total Carbs: 4g, Net Carbs: 3g, Fiber: 1g, Protein: 5g; Sodium: 337mg (1 fat bomb).*

Toast with Cheese and Ham

Ingredients: *(Servings: 2 Prep Time: 5 minutes Cook Time: 6 minutes)*

- 2 slices of keto Italian bread
- 1 tsp. unsalted butter
- 2 slices of cheddar/blue cheese
- 2 slices of Parma ham
- 3 red onion rings
- 2 slices of Roma tomato
- 1 whole egg, cooked

Preparation Method:

1. Heat a skillet over medium heat. Butter one side of both slices of bread and place them butter-side down on the skillet.

2. Add cheese, ham slices, onion rings, and tomato slices to one slice of bread and place the other slice of bread on top.
3. Grill on both sides until the cheese has melted.
4. Serve with fried eggs and fresh summer salad.

Nutrition Per Serve: *Calories: 257, Net Carbs: 18.5 g, Total Carbohydrates: 25.1 g, Total Fat: 9.2 g, Cholesterol 109 mg, Sodium 709 mg, Protein: 20.3 g, Fiber: 6.6 g, Sugar: 7.8 g*

Keto Tortilla Chips

Ingredients: *(Perp time: 10 minutes Serves: 3 Cook time: 15 minutes)*

- 1 cup shredded low-moisture mozzarella cheese
- ½ teaspoon Kosher salt
- ¼ teaspoon chili powder
- ½ cup almond flour
- ½ teaspoon garlic powder
- freshly ground pepper to taste

Preparation Method:

1. Preheat the oven to 350°F. Take a large baking sheet and line it with parchment paper.
2. Place mozzarella cheese in a microwave-safe bowl. Place it in the microwave for about 60 seconds or until it melts. Stir every 20 seconds.
3. Once it completely melts, mix in almond flour, garlic powder, pepper, chili powder, and salt. Mix using your hands until the dough is formed.
4. Place a sheet of parchment paper on your countertop. Place the dough over it. Place another parchment paper over the dough and roll the dough into a rectangle with a thickness of ⅛ inch.
5. Cut into smaller rectangles or triangles. Place the chips on the baking sheet and put it in the oven to bake for 12–15 minutes or until it is slightly crisp.

Nutrition per serve: *Calories: 270 Fat: 22 g Total Carbohydrate: 6 g Net Carbohydrate: 4 g Fiber: 2 g Protein: 15 g (⅓ recipe)*

Salmon-Stuffed Cucumbers

Ingredients: *(Prep Time: 10 minutes Serves 4)*

- 2 large cucumbers, peeled
- 1 (4-ounce) can red salmon
- 1 medium very ripe avocado, mashed
- 1 tablespoon extra-virgin olive oil
- Zest and juice of lime

- 1 lime
- 3 tablespoons chopped fresh cilantro
- ½ teaspoon salt
- ¼ teaspoon freshly ground black pepper

Preparation Method:

1. Slice the cucumber into 1-inch-thick segments and using a spoon, scrape seeds out of center of each segment and stand up on a plate.
2. In a medium bowl, combine the salmon, avocado, olive oil, lime zest and juice, cilantro, salt, and pepper and mix until creamy.
3. Spoon the salmon mixture into the center of each cucumber segment and serve chilled.

Nutrient Per Serving: *Calories: 159, Total Fat: 11g, Total Carbs: 8g, Net Carbs: 5g, Fiber: 3g, Protein: 9g; Sodium: 398mg*

Smoked Salmon Crudités

Ingredients: *(Prep Time: 10 minutes Serves 4)*

- 6 ounces smoked wild salmon
- 2 tablespoons Roasted Garlic Aioli or avocado mayonnaise
- 1 tablespoon Dijon mustard
- 1 tablespoon chopped scallions, green parts only
- 2 teaspoons chopped capers
- ½ teaspoon dried dill
- 4 endive spears or hearts of romaine
- ½ English cucumber, cut into ¼-inch-thick rounds

Preparation Method:

1. Roughly chop the smoked salmon and place in a small bowl. Add the aioli, Dijon, scallions, capers, and dill and mix well.
2. Top endive spears and cucumber rounds with a spoonful of smoked salmon mixture and enjoy chilled.

Nutrition Per Serve: *Calories: 92, Total Fat: 5g, Total Carbs: 5g, Net Carbs: 4g, Fiber: 1g, Protein: 9g; Sodium: 472mg*

Bruschetta Stuffed Avocado

Ingredients: *(Prep time: 5 minutes; Servings: 2 Cook Time: 0 minute)*

- 1 large avocado, pitted and halved
- 3.5-ounce Roma tomato, diced
- 1 tablespoon diced red onion
- 1 tablespoon chopped fresh basil
- ½ teaspoon minced garlic
- ¼ teaspoon salt
- ¼ teaspoon ground black pepper
- 1 teaspoon apple cider vinegar
- 1 tablespoon olive oil

Preparation Method:

1. Place all the ingredients in a bowl except for avocado and stir until mixed.
2. Cut avocado into half, remove its pit and then stuff with prepared bruschetta mixture.
3. Serve immediately.

Nutrition Per Serve: *Calories: 237 Cal, Carbs: 12.1 g, Fat: 21.6 g, Protein: 2.7 g, Fiber: 7.5 g.*

Zucchini-Ricotta Fritters with Lemon-Garlic Aioli

Ingredients: (*Prep Time: 10 minutes Serves 4 Cook Time: 25 minutes*)

- 1 large or 2 small/medium zucchini
- 1 teaspoon salt, divided
- ½ cup whole-milk ricotta cheese
- 2 scallions, chopped
- 1 large egg
- 2 garlic cloves, finely minced
- 2 tablespoons chopped fresh mint (optional)

- 2 teaspoons grated lemon zest
- ¼ teaspoon freshly ground black pepper
- ½ cup almond flour
- 1 teaspoon baking powder
- 8 tablespoons extra-virgin olive oil
- 8 tablespoons Roasted Garlic Aioli

Preparation Method:

1. Place the shredded zucchini in a colander or on several layers of paper towels. Sprinkle with ½ teaspoon salt and let sit for 10 minutes. Using another layer of paper towels, press down on the zucchini to release any excess moisture and pat dry. Don't skip this step or your fritters will be soggy. In a large bowl, combine the drained zucchini, ricotta, scallions, egg, garlic, mint (if using), lemon zest, remaining ½ teaspoon salt, and pepper and stir well.

2. In a small bowl, whisk together the almond flour and baking powder. Stir the flour mixture into the zucchini mixture and let rest for 10 minutes.

3. In a large skillet, working in four batches, fry the fritters. For each batch of four, heat 2 tablespoons olive oil over medium-high heat. Add 1 heaping tablespoon of zucchini batter per fritter, pressing down with the back of a spoon to form 2- to 3-inch fritters. Cover and let fry 2 minutes before flipping. Fry another 2 to 3 minutes, covered, or until crispy and golden and cooked through. You may need to reduce heat to medium to prevent burning. Remove from the pan and keep warm.

4. Repeat for the remaining three batches, using 2 tablespoons of the olive oil for each batch. Serve fritters warm with aioli.

Nutrition Per Serve: *Calories: 448, Total Fat: 42g, Total Carbs: 12g, Net Carbs: 10g, Fiber: 2g, Protein: 8g; Sodium: 713mg (4 fritters with 2 tablespoons aioli)*

Side Dish and Soups Recipes

Artichoke and Tomato Salad

Ingredients: *(Serves: 4 Prep time: 10 minutes Cook time: 0 minutes)*

- 1 can (14 oz.) artichoke hearts, quartered
- 2 cups cherry tomatoes, halved
- 1/4 cup sliced red onion
- 1/4 cup chopped fresh basil

- 2 tbsp. extra-virgin olive oil
- 1 tbsp. lemon juice
- 1 clove garlic, minced
- Salt and black pepper to taste

Preparation Method:

1 In a large bowl, combine artichoke hearts, cherry tomatoes, red onion, and fresh basil.
2 In a small bowl, whisk together olive oil, lemon juice, garlic, salt, and black pepper to make the dressing.
3 Pour the dressing over the salad ingredients and toss to coat evenly.
4 Serve chilled or at room temperature.

Nutrition Per Serve: *Calories: 110 Protein: 3g Carbohydrates: 10g Fat: 7g Fiber: 4g Cholesterol: 0mg Sodium: 290mg Potassium: 430mg*

Avocado Gazpacho

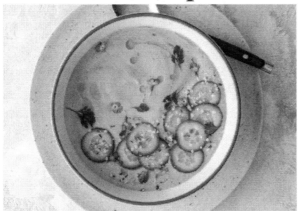

Ingredients: *(Prep Time: 15 minutes Serves 4)*

- 2 cups chopped tomatoes
- 2 large ripe avocados, halved and pitted
- 1 large cucumber, peeled and seeded
- 1 medium bell pepper (red, orange or yellow), chopped
- 1 cup plain whole-milk Greek yogurt
- ¼ cup extra-virgin olive oil
- ¼ cup chopped fresh cilantro
- ¼ cup chopped scallions, green part only
- 2 tablespoons red wine vinegar
- Juice of 2 limes or 1 lemon
- ½ to 1 teaspoon salt
- ¼ teaspoon freshly ground black pepper

Preparation Method:

1. In a blender or in a large bowl, if using an immersion blender, combine the tomatoes, avocados, cucumber, bell pepper, yogurt, olive oil, cilantro, scallions, vinegar, and lime juice. Blend until smooth.
2. Season with salt and pepper and blend to combine the flavors.
3. Chill in the refrigerator for 1 to 2 hours before serving. Serve cold.

Nutrition Per Serve: *Calories: 392, Total Fat: 32g, Total Carbs: 20g, Net Carbs: 11g, Fiber: 9g, Protein: 6g; Sodium: 335mg*

Cauliflower Parmesan Soup

Ingredients: *(Prep Time: 5 minutes; Servings: 6; Cook Time: 35 minutes)*

- 1 medium head of cauliflower, florets chopped
- 1/2 of medium white onion, peeled and sliced
- ½ of medium leek, sliced
- 4 tablespoons unsalted butter
- ¾ teaspoon salt

- ½ teaspoon cracked black pepper
- 2 tablespoons fresh thyme, chopped
- 4 tablespoons olive oil
- 1 cup grated parmesan cheese, full-fat
- 2 cups vegetable broth
- 3 cups water

Preparation Method:

1. Place a large pot over medium heat, add 2 tablespoons butter and cook until melt completely.
2. Then add onion, leek, and salt and cook for 3 to 5 minutes or until softened. Add half of the chopped cauliflower florets, oil, vegetable broth, and water and stir until mixed.
3. Bring the mixture to simmer and cook for 15 minutes or until cauliflower is tender. Stir in a ¾ portion of remaining cauliflower florets into the pot and continue simmering until tender.
4. In the meantime, place a frying pan over medium heat, add remaining butter, remaining chopped cauliflower florets and thyme and cook for 3 to 5 minutes or until butter starts to bubble, and cauliflower is nicely golden brown.
5. When cauliflower is cook, remove the pot from heat and blend with a stick blender until smooth. Top soup with browned cauliflower and serves.

Nutrition Per Serve: *Calories: 240 Cal, Carbs: 7 g, Fat: 20 g, Protein: 8 g, Fiber: 3 g.*

Cheesy Cauliflower Mash

Ingredients: *(Prep time: 5 minutes Serves: 2 Cook Time: 6 minutes)*

- ½ large head cauliflower, cut into florets
- ½ tablespoon butter
- 1-ounce sharp cheddar cheese
- 1 tablespoon heavy cream
- salt to taste
- A large pinch of garlic powder
- Pepper to taste

Preparation Method:

1. Combine butter, cream, and garlic powder in a microwave-safe bowl.
2. Place in the microwave and cook on high for 2 minutes.
3. Add cauliflower and stir. Cook for 5–6 minutes or until fork tender.
4. Blend the cauliflower mixture until smooth, adding cheese, salt, and pepper while blending.
5. Pour into a bowl and keep warm until ready to serve.

Nutrition Per Serve: *Calories: 167 Fat: 11 g Total Carbohydrate: 12.05 g Net Carbohydrate: 7.65 g Fiber: 4.4 g Protein: 6 g*

Chicken Zoodle Soup

Ingredients: *(Prep time: 15 minutes Serves: 4 Cook time: 25 minutes)*

- 1 tbsp olive oil
- 1 onion, diced
- 2 cloves garlic, minced
- 2 carrots, sliced
- 2 celery stalks, sliced
- 4cups chicken broth
- 1 can diced tomatoes (14 oz)
- 1 tsp dried oregano

- 1/2 tsp dried thyme
- 1/2 tsp dried rosemary
- Salt and pepper to taste
- 1 lb cooked, shredded chicken breasts
- 2 medium zucchini, spiralized into zoodles
- Juice of 1 lemon
- Fresh parsley, chopped (for garnish)

Preparation Method:

1. Heat olive oil in a large pot. Sauté onion and garlic. Add carrots and celery, cook until slightly softened.
2. Pour in chicken broth, diced tomatoes, and spices. Simmer for 15 minutes.
3. Add shredded chicken and simmer for 5 minutes.
4. Add zucchini noodles and cook for 2-3 minutes. Stir in lemon juice. Adjust seasonings if needed.
5. Serve hot, garnished with fresh parsley.

Nutrition Per Serve: *Calories: 220 Protein: 25g Carbs: 12g Fat: 8g Fiber: 4g Cholesterol: 55mg Sodium: 800mg Potassium: 900mg*

Cream of Cauliflower Gazpacho

Ingredients: *(Prep Time: 15 minutes Serves 4 to 6 Cook Time: 25 minutes)*

- 1 cup raw almonds
- ½ teaspoon salt
- ½ cup extra-virgin olive oil, plus 1 tablespoon, divided
- 1 small white onion, minced

- 1 small (3 cups) head cauliflower, broken into florets
- 2 garlic cloves, finely minced
- 2 cups chicken or vegetable stock
- 1 tablespoon red wine vinegar
- ¼ teaspoon freshly

- ground black pepper

Preparation Method:

1   Bring a small pot of water to a boil. Add the almonds to the water and boil for 1 minute. Drain in a colander and run under cold water. Pat dry and, using your fingers, squeeze the meat of each almond out of its skin. Discard the skins.

2   In a food processor or blender, blend together the almonds and salt. With the processor running, drizzle in ½ cup extra-virgin olive oil, scraping down the sides as needed. Set the almond paste aside.

3   In a large stockpot, heat the remaining 1 tablespoon olive oil over medium-high heat. Add the onion and sauté until golden, 3 to 4 minutes. Add the cauliflower florets and sauté for another 3 to 4 minutes. Add the garlic and sauté for 1 minute more.

4   Add 2 cups stock and bring to a boil. Cover, reduce the heat to medium-low, and simmer the vegetables until tender, 8 to 10 minutes. Remove from the heat and allow to cool slightly.

5   Add the vinegar and pepper. Using an immersion blender, blend until smooth. With the blender running, add the almond paste and blend until smooth, adding extra stock if the soup is too thick.

6   Serve warm, or chill in refrigerator at least 4 to 6 hours to serve a cold gazpacho.

Nutrition Per Serve: *Calories: 505, Total Fat: 45g, Total Carbs: 15g, Net Carbs: 10g, Fiber: 5g, Protein: 10g; Sodium: 484mg*

Cucumber Soup

Ingredients: *(Prep time: 2 hours and 5 minutes; Serves: 6 Cook Time: 0 minutes)*

- 4-pound cucumbers, chopped
- 1 medium cucumber, sliced
- 2 medium avocados
- 2 tablespoons chopped basil leaves and more for topping
- 2 large spring onions, chopped
- 1 teaspoon minced garlic
- 3/4 teaspoon sea salt
- 1/4 teaspoon cracked black pepper
- 3 tablespoons lime juice
- 1/2 cup olive oil, divided
- 2 cups chicken stock
- 1 medium cucumber, thinly sliced

Preparation Method:

1 Place chopped cucumber in a blender, add avocado, onion, garlic, basil, salt, black pepper, lime juice, olive oil, and water.
2 Pulse for 2 minutes at high speed or until smooth and creamy and then pour this mixture into a saucepan.
3 Place the saucepan into the refrigerator for 2 hours or until chilled.
4 When ready to serve, ladle soup into bowls, top with sliced cucumber and basil and serve.

Nutrition Per Serve: *Calories: 266 Cal, Carbs: 9.5 g, Fat: 25.7 g, Protein: 2.4 g, Fiber: 4.9 g.*

Creamy Wild Mushroom Soup

Ingredients: *(Prep Time: 15 minutes Serves 8 Cook Time: 1 hour)*

- 1 cup (1.1 oz) dried porcini mushrooms and/or morel mushrooms
- 2 cups boiling water
- ½ medium (12.4 oz) cauliflower, cut into florets and sliced
- 1 small (2.1 oz) red onion, roughly chopped
- 2 cloves garlic, halved
- ¼ cup extra-virgin avocado oil

- 3cups chicken stock
- 12 ounces' brown mushrooms
- Few sprigs fresh thyme, leaves only, or 1 teaspoon dried thyme
- 1 cup coconut cream, goat's cream, or heavy whipping cream
- ½ cup extra-virgin olive oil, to drizzle
- Fresh thyme sprigs, to serve

Optional:

sour cream, coconut yogurt, or coconut cream, to serve

Preparation Method:

1. Place the dried mushrooms in a small bowl and pour over enough boiling water to cover them. Set aside to soak for about 30 minutes. Preheat the oven to 355°F (180°C) fan assisted or 400°F (200°C) conventional.
2. Place the cauliflower florets, onion, and garlic on a baking tray. Drizzle with the avocado oil or ghee and bake for about 30 minutes. Remove from the oven and set aside.
3. Meanwhile, pour the chicken stock into a large pot and bring to a boil. Add the cauliflower mixture, soaked porcini mushrooms, and fresh mushrooms.
4. Cook for about 8 minutes, until the mushrooms are tender. Add the thyme and coconut cream and heat through. Remove from the heat and set aside to cool for a few minutes.
5. Use an immersion blender, or pour into a blender, to process until smooth and creamy. If the soup is too thick, add water or more stock until the desired consistency is reached.
6. To serve, pour into serving bowls and drizzle each with the olive oil. Garnish with more thyme and serve with a dollop of sour cream, if using.

Nutrition Per Serving: *Total carbs: 9.8 g Fiber: 2.4 g Net Carbs: 7.4 g Protein: 5.3 g Fat: 32.9 g (of which saturated: 12.9 g) Calories: 340 kcal*

Dilled Tuna Salad Sandwich

Ingredients: *(Prep Time: 10 minutes Serves 4 Cook time: 20 minutes)*

- 4 Versatile Sandwich Rounds
- 2 (4-ounce) cans tuna, packed in olive oil
- 2 tablespoons Roasted Garlic Aioli
- 1 to 2 teaspoons freshly squeezed lemon juice and/or zest

- 1 very ripe avocado, peeled, pitted, and mashed
- 1 tablespoon chopped fresh capers (optional)
- 1 teaspoon chopped fresh dill or ½ teaspoon dried dill

Preparation Method:

1. Make sandwich rounds according to recipe. Cut each round in half and set aside.
2. In a medium bowl, place the tuna and the oil from cans. Add the aioli, avocado, capers (if using), and dill and blend well with a fork.
3. Toast sandwich rounds and fill each with one-quarter of the tuna salad, about ⅓ cup.

Nutrition Per Serve: *Calories: 436, Total Fat: 36g, Total Carbs: 5g, Net Carbs: 2g, Fiber: 3g, Protein: 23g; Sodium: 790mg (1 sandwich)*

Eggplant and Tomato Stacks with Mozzarella

Ingredients: (Serves: 4 Prep time: 15 minutes Cook time: 20 minutes)

- 1 large eggplant
- 2 large tomatoes
- 8ounces' fresh mozzarella cheese
- 2 tablespoons olive oil

- 2 cloves garlic, minced
- 1 teaspoon dried basil
- Salt and pepper, to taste
- Fresh basil leaves, for garnish (optional)

Preparation Method:

1   Preheat oven to 400°F (200°C). Line a baking sheet with parchment paper. Slice eggplant and tomatoes into 1/4-inch rounds.
2   Place eggplant on baking sheet, brush with olive oil, and sprinkle with garlic, dried basil, salt, and pepper.
3   Bake for 15-20 minutes until tender and golden brown. Layer eggplant, tomato, and mozzarella to create stacks.
4   Return stacks to the oven for 5 minutes until cheese melts.
5   Garnish with fresh basil leaves, if desired. Serve warm.

Nutrition Per Serve: *Calories: 210 Protein: 12g Carbohydrates: 11g Fat: 14g Fiber: 4g Cholesterol: 30mg Sodium: 270mg Potassium: 520mg*

Faux Potato Salad

Ingredients: *(Prep Time: 10 minutes Serves 2 Cook Time: 10 minutes)*

- ½ pound cauliflower
- ½ tablespoon olive oil
- ½ tablespoon Dijon mustard
- ⅛ teaspoon paprika
- ⅛ teaspoon sea salt
- 1 hard-boiled egg, peeled, chopped

- 3 tablespoons keto-friendly mayonnaise
- 1 tablespoon white vinegar
- ½ teaspoon garlic powder
- ⅛ teaspoon celery salt
- ⅛ teaspoon pepper
- ⅛ cup chopped scallions

Directions:

1. Pour about 2 inches of water into a pot or saucepan. Place a steamer basket in it. Place cauliflower in the basket and cover it with a lid.
2. Steam for 10 minutes or until tender, and you are able to pierce easily with a fork. Allow it to cool completely.
3. Combine cauliflower, egg, onion, and scallion in a bowl.
4. To make the dressing: Whisk together oil, mustard, paprika, salt, vinegar, garlic powder, celery salt, and pepper in a bowl.
5. Pour the dressing over the salad and toss well. Cover the bowl and refrigerate until you need to serve.

Nutrition Per Serve: *Calories: 227 Fat: 20 g Total Carbohydrate: 7 g Net Carbohydrate: 5 g Fiber: 2 g Protein: 5 g*

Greek Chicken and "Rice" Soup with Artichokes

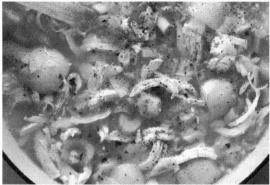

Ingredients: *(Prep Time: 10 minutes Serves 4 Cook Time: 15 minutes)*

- cups Chicken Stock
- 2 cups Riced Cauliflower, divided
- 2 large egg yolks
- ¼ cup freshly squeezed lemon juice
- ¾ cup extra-virgin olive oil, divided
- 8 ounces cooked chicken, coarsely chopped
- 1 (13.75-ounce) can artichoke hearts, drained and quartered
- ¼ cup chopped fresh dill

Preparation Method:

1. In a large saucepan, bring the stock to a low boil. Reduce the heat to low and simmer, covered.
2. Transfer 1 cup of the hot stock to a blender or food processor. Add ½ cup raw riced cauliflower, the egg yolks, and lemon juice and purée. While the blending, stream in ½ cup olive oil and blend until smooth.
3. Whisking constantly, pour the purée into the simmering stock until well blended together and smooth.
4. Add the chicken and artichokes and simmer until thickened slightly, 8 to 10 minutes. Stir in the dill and remaining 1½ cups riced cauliflower.
5. Serve warm, drizzled with the remaining ¼ cup olive oil.

Nutrition Per Serve: *Calories: 566, Total Fat: 46g, Total Carbs: 14g, Net Carbs: 7g, Fiber: 7g, Protein: 24g; Sodium: 754mg*

Greek Lentil Soup with Spinach and Lemon

Ingredients: *(Prep time: 10 minutes Serves: 4 Cook time: 40 minutes)*

- 1 cup green lentils
- 1 onion, chopped
- 2 cloves garlic, minced
- 2 carrots, diced
- 2 celery stalks, diced
- 4cups vegetable broth
- 1 bay leaf
- 1 tsp dried oregano
- 1 tsp dried thyme
- 4cups fresh spinach leaves
- Juice of 1 lemon
- Salt and pepper to taste
- Olive oil for drizzling

Preparation Method:

1. Rinse the lentils under cold water and set aside. In a large pot, heat olive oil over medium heat.
2. Add the onion, garlic, carrots, and celery.
3. Sauté until vegetables are tender. Add the lentils, vegetable broth, bay leaf, oregano, and thyme to the pot.
4. Bring to a boil, then reduce heat and simmer for 30 minutes or until lentils are cooked. Stir in the spinach and cook for an additional 5 minutes until wilted.
5. Remove the bay leaf and stir in the lemon juice. Season with salt and pepper to taste.
6. Ladle the soup into bowls and drizzle with olive oil before serving.

Nutrition Per Serve: *Calories: 250 Protein: 15g Carbohydrates: 40g Fat: 4g Fiber: 15g Cholesterol: 0mg Sodium: 800mg Potassium: 1000mg*

Lemon Garlic Roasted Broccoli

Ingredients: (Prep time: 5 minutes Serves: 4 Cook time: 20 minutes)

- 1 head of broccoli, cut into florets
- 2 tablespoons olive oil
- 2 cloves garlic, minced
- 1 tablespoon lemon juice
- Zest of 1 lemon
- Salt and black pepper to taste

Preparation Method:

1. Preheat the oven to 425°F (220°C) and line a baking sheet with parchment paper.
2. In a large bowl, toss the broccoli florets with olive oil, minced garlic, lemon juice, lemon zest, salt, and black pepper.
3. Spread the seasoned broccoli in a single layer on the prepared baking sheet.
4. Roast in the preheated oven for about 20 minutes, or until the broccoli is tender and lightly browned, stirring halfway through cooking.
5. Remove from the oven and serve hot.

Nutrition Per Serve: *Calories: 90 Protein: 4g Carbohydrates: 8g Fat: 6g Fiber: 3g Cholesterol: 0mg Sodium: 50mg Potassium: 470mg*

Orange-Tarragon Chicken Salad Wrap

Ingredients: (Prep Time: 15 minutes Serves 4 Cook time: 0 minutes)

- ½ cup plain whole-milk Greek yogurt
- 2 tablespoons Dijon mustard
- 2 tablespoons extra-virgin olive oil
- 2 tablespoons chopped fresh tarragon or 1 teaspoon dried tarragon
- ½ teaspoon salt
- ¼ teaspoon freshly ground black pepper
- 2 cups cooked shredded chicken ½ cup slivered almonds
- 4to 8 large lettuce leaves, tough stem removed
- 2 small ripe avocados, thinly sliced
- Zest of 1 clementine, or ½ small orange (1 tablespoon)

Preparation Method:

1 In a medium bowl, combine the yogurt, mustard, olive oil, tarragon, orange zest, salt, and pepper and whisk until creamy.
2 Add the shredded chicken and almonds and stir to coat
3 To assemble the wraps, place about ½ cup chicken salad mixture in the center of each lettuce leaf and top with sliced avocados.

Nutrition Per Serve: *Calories: 440, Total Fat: 32g, Total Carbs: 12g, Net Carbs: 4g, Fiber: 8g, Protein: 26g; Sodium: 445mg*

Roasted Cauliflower with Garlic and Lemon

Ingredients: *(Prep time: 10 minutes Serves: 4 Cook time: 25 minutes)*

- 1 large head of cauliflower, cut into florets
- 3tablespoons olive oil
- 4cloves garlic, minced
- Zest of 1 lemon

- Juice of 1 lemon
- 1 teaspoon dried thyme
- Salt and black pepper to taste
- Fresh parsley, chopped (for garnish)

Preparation Method:

1 Preheat the oven to 425°F (220°C) and line a baking sheet with parchment paper.
2 In a large bowl, combine the cauliflower florets, olive oil, minced garlic, lemon zest, lemon juice, dried thyme, salt, and black pepper.
3 Toss until the cauliflower is evenly coated. Spread the cauliflower in a single layer on the prepared baking sheet.
4 Roast in the preheated oven for 20-25 minutes, or until the cauliflower is tender and lightly browned, stirring once halfway through.
5 Remove from the oven and transfer the roasted cauliflower to a serving dish.
6 Garnish with fresh chopped parsley. Serve hot as a delicious side dish.

Nutritional Per Serve: *Calories: 120 Protein: 5g Carbohydrates: 10g Fat: 8g Fiber: 4g Cholesterol: 0mg Sodium: 80mg Potassium: 560mg*

Spanish Tomato Soup

Ingredients: *(Prep Time: 10 minutes Serves: 6 Cook Time: 20 minutes)*

- 27 oz. canned, whole peeled tomatoes
- 3Tbsp. dried onion flakes
- 1 cup celery, finely chopped
- 2 garlic cloves, minced
- ¼ cup fresh basil leaves
- 2 Tbsp. olive oil
- ½ cup pecans
- ½ tsp. kosher salt
- 2 Tbsp. tomato paste
- 2 cups vegetable broth

Preparation Method:

1. To a large pot over medium heat, add celery, garlic, olive oil, onion flakes, and salt. Sauté for 7–8 minutes until the celery is softened. Stir in tomato paste.
2. Add the canned tomatoes and bring to a mellow simmer. Allow the soup to simmer uncovered for 10 minutes.
3. Transfer the soup to a food processor or high-speed blender, adding the pecans and basil at the same time. Blend until smooth.
4. Serve with mozzarella balls, boiled eggs, chopped ham, and crispy bread.

Nutrition Per Serve: *Calories: 288, Net Carbs: 7.8 g, Total Carbohydrates: 13 g, Total Fat 25.5 g, Sodium 280 mg, Dietary Fiber: 5.2 g, Total Sugars: 6 g*

Tomato and Mozzarella Caprese Salad

Ingredients: *(Prep time: 10 minutes Serves: 4 Cook time: 0 minutes)*

- 4medium tomatoes, sliced
- 8ounces' fresh mozzarella cheese, sliced
- 1/4 cup fresh basil leaves

- 2 tablespoons extra virgin olive oil
- 1 tablespoon balsamic vinegar
- Salt and black pepper to taste

Preparation Method:

1. Arrange the tomato slices and mozzarella slices on a serving platter, alternating between them.
2. Tuck the fresh basil leaves in between the tomato and mozzarella slices.
3. Drizzle the extra virgin olive oil and balsamic vinegar over the salad. Sprinkle salt and black pepper to taste.
4. Allow the flavors to meld together for a few minutes before serving.
5. Serve the tomato and mozzarella Caprese salad as a refreshing and light side dish.

Nutrition Per Serve: *Calories: 220 Protein: 11g Carbohydrates: 6g Fat: 17g Fiber: 1g Cholesterol: 30mg Sodium: 280mg Potassium: 350mg*

Traditional Greek Salad

Ingredients: (Prep Time: 10 minutes Serves 4 Cook Time: 20 minutes)

- 2 large English cucumbers
- 4Roma tomatoes, quartered
- 1 green bell pepper, cut into 1- to 1½-inch chunks
- ¼ small red onion, thinly sliced
- 4ounces pitted Kalamata olives
- ¼ cup extra-virgin olive oil
- 2 tablespoons freshly squeezed lemon juice

- 1 tablespoon red wine vinegar
- 1 tablespoon chopped fresh oregano or 1 teaspoon dried oregano
- ¼ teaspoon freshly ground black pepper
- 4ounces crumbled traditional feta cheese

Preparation Method:

1. Cut the cucumbers in half lengthwise and then into ½-inch-thick half-moons. Place in a large bowl.
2. Add the quartered tomatoes, bell pepper, red onion, and olives.
3. In a small bowl, whisk together the olive oil, lemon juice, vinegar, oregano, and pepper. Drizzle over the vegetables and toss to coat.
4. Divide between salad plates and top each with 1 ounce of feta.

Nutrition Per Serve: *Calories: 278, Total Fat: 22g, Total Carbs: 12g, Net Carbs: 8g, Fiber: 4g, Protein: 8g; Sodium: 572mg*

Tuscan White Bean Soup

Ingredients: *(Prep Time: 10 minutes Serve: 8 Cook Time: 20 minutes)*

- 30 oz can cannellini beans, drained and rinsed
- ½ tsp paprika
- 1 tsp dried basil
- ½ tsp red pepper flakes
- 2 cups water

- 4cups vegetable broth
- 2 (28 oz.) cans tomatoes, diced
- 2 tbsp. olive oil
- 2 bunches Tuscan kale, chopped
- 1 bulb fennel, chopped
- Pepper and Salt, as required

Preparation Method:

1. Heat olive oil in a large pot over medium-high heat.
2. Add fennel to the pot and sauté for 5 minutes.
3. Add tomatoes and cook for 8 minutes.
4. Add beans, water, and vegetable broth and bring to a boil.
5. Turn heat to low, simmer, and add paprika, basil, red pepper flakes, and salt.
6. Add kale, stir well and cook for 5 minutes. Stir well and serve.

Nutrition Per Serve: *Calories 172 Fat 5 g Carbohydrates 23 g Sugar 5 g Protein 9 g Cholesterol 0 mg*

Summary

The Mediterranean Ketogenic diet is a journey that brings the best diet of two different worlds together; the heart-healthy Mediterranean diet and the ketogenic diet and lifestyle. The ancient lifestyle of the Mediterranean has incredible benefits like improving overall body health, prevention of heart diseases, weight loss, acne reduction, relief from PCOS, and potential alleviation of various cancers. Its resurgence to provided incredible hope for helping cure epileptic fits and re-gaining energy.

On the other hand, the ketogenic diet is a method to refuel your body through ketones instead of carbs. A simple change in fuel can bring incredible transformations to your metabolism. You are also aware of the risks of the keto diet and the precautions you need to take to be successful in your fitness journey.

The Mediterranean Ketogenic fusion aims to strike a balance between the traditional Mediterranean diet's focus on fresh, locally sourced ingredients and the low-carb, high-fat principles of the Ketogenic diet. By doing so, it offers potential health benefits such as improved cardiovascular health, better blood sugar control, and weight management, while still allowing for the enjoyment of flavorful and diverse foods.

However, the fusion promotes both heart-healthy, nutrient-rich foods and the metabolic benefits of ketosis. This diet emphasizes the consumption of whole foods like vegetables, fruits, nuts, seeds, and olive oil, which are staples of the Mediterranean diet and known for their heart-healthy properties. At the same time, it restricts carbohydrates to induce a state of ketosis, where the body burns fat for fuel instead of glucose. This can help with weight loss and may have potential benefits for managing some heat conditions.

There is also the comprehensive collection of delicious homemade recipes that combine the rich flavors and vibrant ingredients of the Mediterranean region with the principles of the ketogenic diet, promoting both flavor and healthy living. It also explores the Mediterranean-inspired keto recipes for breakfast, lunch, dinner, and even snacks and side dish.

The wide range of recipes showcase the fusion of flavors from avocado toast to zesty Greek salads with feta cheese to succulent grilled lamb chops with garlic and rosemary, these dishes offer an explosion of taste without compromising your diet goals. Each recipes comes with a comprehensive nutritional fact that, provide information including net carb counts, fat content, and protein levels, to make it easier to track your macros and stay in ketosis.

A Thirty-Day Plan

Over the previous chapters, a massive database of diverse recipes has been provided for your needs. However, there might be challenges of beginning a new diet and that sometimes it can be overwhelming to take the first step. To make things easier, this chapter will guide you through a thirty-day plan. The chapter will provide a clear-cut chart for what to eat when to eat, what ingredients to buy, and how to cope with the stock. It will help you make yourself comfortable with this lifestyle change before you begin experimenting in the kitchen. Of course, you are free to use any of the recipes provided in the earlier chapters. But the purpose of having a time-set plan is to track your progress. If you have been doubting your ability to stick to a new diet, or stressing about how you will prepare your meals, do not worry. This chapter will clarify all your self-doubt and help you accomplish your health goals.

Now it's time to get started! the meal plan is designed to fit the ideal macronutrient ratios for a successful transition into ketosis using the wide variety of delicious recipes found in this book. However, feel free to adjust the amount of cooking to fit your needs and preferences. Some people need a lot of variety in their meals and don't enjoy eating the same thing twice. Others tend to thrive on routine and, once they find a breakfast or lunch that works, they don't mind having that every day to keep things simple. Do whatever work best for you.

About the Meal Plans

Many recipes can be made in advance to free up your time during the week, and some meals will have leftovers that will be eaten again during the week (or in the following week). You'll also find a shopping list with all the fresh ingredients you'll need. If you decide to double up recipes and omit others, you will need to modify these shopping lists. Snack options are included, but they are there only if you feel hungry between meals. The ingredients for the snacks are not included on the shopping lists, so be sure to add them if you plan on making them. Snacks are helpful during the first week, when your body has not fully transitioned into ketosis. However, as your body adjusts, you will likely begin to feel more satiety and less need for snacking, which is a great sign your body is making a metabolic shift. Part of this process is learning to listen to your body, and if you don't feel the need for snacks, then by all means omit them. The weekly plans include a "breakfast" meal, a heavier afternoon "lunch," "snacks" and a "dinner." As you stick to the schedule of the weekdays, pushing breakfast later may come naturally as you enter ketosis and feel more satiated from the higher-fat and filling meals.

Week 1

Days	Breakfast	Lunch	Snacks and Appetizer	Dinner
1	Avocado Toast	Asparagus Salmon Fillets	Stuffed Mushrooms	Turkey Chorizo with Bok Choy
2	Caprese Omelet	Zucchini Pizza	Toast with Cheese and Ham	Pork Cutlets in Cucumber Sauce
3	Asparagus Frittata	Spinach Chicken	Burrata Caprese Stack	Brie-Stuffed Meatballs
4	Chicken Casserole	Bacon, Lettuce, and Tomato Stuffed Avocado	Zucchini-Ricotta Fritters with Lemon-Garlic Aioli	White Fish Casserole
5	Skewers with Halloumi Cheese and Cherry Tomatoes	Club Sandwich	Salmon-Stuffed Cucumbers	Creamy Chicken Stew
6	Egg Muffins	Shrimp Scampi Zoodles	Flavored Roasted Seed and Nut Mix	Authentic Turkey Kebabs
7	Olive & Herb Focaccia	Greek Cauliflower Rice	Goat Cheese–Mackerel Pâté	Spicy Chicken Breasts

Week 2

Days	Breakfast	Lunch	Snacks and Appetizer	Dinner
8	Breakfast Muffins	Sour and Sweet Fish	Citrus-Marinated Olives	Chicken Stew with Vegetables
9	Egg Salad Lettuce Wraps	Paprika Butter Shrimp	Manchego Crackers	Parmesan-Crusted Pork
10	Bruschetta with Avocado and Salmon	White Fish with Lemon	Classic Stuffed Mushrooms	Coconut Shrimp Skillet
11	Savory Pancake	Caprese Stuffed Portobello Mushrooms	Artichoke and Spinach Dip	Flatbread with Chicken Liver Pâté
12	Pesto Scrambled Eggs	Feta Cheese Stuffed Bell Peppers	Grilled Portobello Mushrooms	Lamb Chops Curry
13	Spinach and Feta Crustless Quiche	Crispy Ginger Mackerel Lunch Bowls	Mashed Roasted Eggplant with Spice (Ghanoush)	Old-Fashioned Goulash
14	Sicilian Caponata	Lemongrass Prawns	Roasted Vegetable Balls	Sunday Chicken with Cauliflower Salad

Week 3

Days	Breakfast	Lunch	Snacks and Appetizer	Dinner
15	Blueberry Power Smoothie	Roasted Garlic Shrimp	Cauliflower Falafel	Pork Tenderloin
16	Smoked Salmon and Cream Cheese Rolls	Creamy Chicken	The Mediterranean Fat Bombs	Golden Scallops
17	Keto Greek Yogurt Smoothie with Cucumber and Mint	Tuna Fishcakes	Keto Tortilla Chips	Pork Spare Ribs
18	French Gratin with Cheese Crust	Honey Glazed Chicken Drumsticks	Greek Deviled Eggs	Grilled Lamb Chops
19	Spinach Wrap	Salmon Burgers	Smoked Salmon Crudités	Roasted Leg Lamb
20	Chicken Casserole	Crispy Baked Chicken	Olive Tapenade with Anchovies	Sirloin Beef Roast
21	Egg Muffins	Creamy Chicken	Burrata Caprese Stack	Brie-Stuffed Meatballs

Week 4

Days	Breakfast	Lunch	Snacks and Appetizer	Dinner
22	Mushroom Frittata with Parmesan	Greek Cauliflower Rice	Flavored Roasted Seed and Nut Mix	Spicy Chicken Breasts
23	Asparagus Frittata	Lemongrass Prawns	Manchego Crackers	Coconut Shrimp Skillet
24	Spinach and Feta Crustless Quiche	Shrimp Scampi Zoodles	Grilled Portobello Mushrooms	Pork Tenderloin
25	Egg Salad Lettuce Wraps	Spinach Chicken	Cauliflower Falafel	Authentic Turkey Kebabs
26	Bruschetta with Avocado and Salmon	Crispy Baked Chicken	Greek Deviled Eggs	Old-Fashioned Goulash
27	French Gratin with Cheese Crust	Feta Cheese Stuffed Bell Peppers	Manchego Crackers	Flatbread with Chicken Liver Pâté
28	Chicken Casserole	Tuna Fishcakes	Salmon-Stuffed Cucumbers	Lamb Chops Curry

Week 5

Days	Breakfast	Lunch	Snacks and Appetizer	Dinner
29	Breakfast Muffins	Shrimp Scampi Zoodles	Goat Cheese–Mackerel Pâté	Creamy Chicken Stew
30	Savory Pancake	Lemongrass Prawns	Greek Deviled Eggs	Coconut Shrimp Skillet

Grocery Shopping List

Where to Find Ingredients

The recipes provided are vast and diverse. As mentioned in previous chapters, keto is successful only when you eat clean ingredients. Sometimes it can be challenging to differentiate between good and harmful ingredients. You might want a packet of cheese to add to your breakfast or fresh vegetables for your frittata. Meat and eggs, too, come in many packaged forms. But you need to be careful about what you're buying because some companies add preservatives and hormones to food that might harm your health. To help you access the best quality ingredients, I have provided a list of places and markets you should visit to fill your shopping cart.

1 **Local Farmers Market:** You should seek weekly markets for vegetables, poultry, herbs, and spices. Cultivators set up stalls that sell supplies directly sourced from farms. This ensures that the least number of preservatives have gone into making the product. Items found here are also cheaper and of better quality. The best time to get your hands on the freshest produce is to wake up early and hit your local farmer's market.

2 **Walmart:** Often it can be difficult to visit the local market and search for fresh produce due to a hectic schedule. Multi-specialty stores like Walmart come in handy when you want to purchase ingredients quickly. The best part is that there is a variety of options you can pick from depending on your preferences. You can use one of the macro tracking apps mentioned in earlier chapters to scan the barcode of each item you want to purchase. Not only can you track nutritional value but compare different products to make the best choice.

3 **Online Apps:** The twenty-first century has seen the rise of online shopping. You can get your daily groceries delivered in the comfort of your home. A quick google search will help you find multiple online stores that cater to your needs. The best part about ordering online is that you can get your ingredients delivered within thirty minutes. So, if you have been craving a specific ingredient but do not have the time to drive to a store, you know what to do.

Shopping Lists

Fish and Sea Food:

- Mackerel (canned)
- Prawns
- Salmon (such as cod or haddock)
- Salmon fillets
- Shrimp
- Tuna (canned or fresh)
- White fish (2 cod/hake/tilapia/haddock)

Vegetables:

- Artichoke
- Asparagus
- Basil leaves
- Bell pepper (green, red and yellow)
- Bok choy
- Broccoli
- Brussels sprouts
- Butternut squash
- Cauliflower
- Cayenne pepper
- Chives
- Cilantro
- Cinnamon
- Cucumbers
- Lettuce leaves
- Mint leaves
- Mushrooms
- Spinach
- Tomatoes
- Zucchini\Eggplant

Proteins:

- Bacon

- lamb (loin, leg)
- Chicken (breasts, grounded, fillets, wing)
- Eggs
- Pork (tenderloin)
- Turkey (breasts, grounded, fillets

Fruits:

- Avocado
- Berries (strawberries, blueberries, raspberries)
- Kalamata olives
- Paprika
- Sage
- Zucchini

Dairy and Dairy Alternatives:

- Almond milk (unsweetened)
- Butter
- Coconut cream (canned, unsweetened)
- Greek yogurt (full-fat, unsweetened)
- Cheese (Halloumi, Mozzarella, Parmesan, Feta, Brie)
- Heavy cream
- Milk

Herbs and Spices:

- Apple cider vinegar
- Basil
- Cilantro
- Cumin
- Curry powder
- Garlic
- Garlic powder
- Ginger
- Green onions
- Ground black pepper

- Herbs de Provence
- Italian herbs
- Mint
- Onion
- Oregano
- Paprika
- Parsley
- Red pepper flakes
- Rosemary
- Thyme
- Turmeric
- Turmeric powder

Nuts and Seeds:

- Almonds
- Anise seeds
- Caraway seeds
- Flaxseeds
- Pine nuts
- Walnuts

Oils and Fats:

- Avocado oil
- Coconut oil
- Olive oil (extra virgin)

Pantry Staples:

- Almond flour
- Baking powder
- Cauliflower rice (frozen or pre-riced)
- Coconut flour

Miscellaneous:

- Honey
- Lemon juice
- Lime juice
- Mayonnaise
- Olives (green and black)
- Pickles
- Red wine vinegar
- White wine

Conclusion

Thank you for reading so far!

Over the previous chapters, you have learnt about the Mediterranean ketogenic diet, its benefits, and the diverse recipes you can play with to kick-start your health journey. Indeed, Mediterranean Ketogenic diet is the quickest way to attaining a healthy life style. The diet is evident for its amazing health benefits, especially physical fitness.

Following a diet shouldn't always be consuming healthy foods that is high in fats. One should also have a healthy lifestyle like adopting quality habits that create positive impacts on mind, heart, and soul. You can achieve the best of these both worlds by following Ketogenic diet influenced with the Mediterranean diet.

By embracing the diet, you are not only embarking on a path towards improved health and vitality but also savoring the joys of diverse and delicious dishes. This book will also serve as your trusted companion on your health journey, providing a collection of recipes that cater to your taste buds and nourish your body.

Remember, this cookbook is more than just a collection of recipes; it's a testament to the idea that eating well should never mean compromising on taste. With its carefully crafted recipes and a wealth of nutritional knowledge, this cookbook will arm you with the tools necessary to transform your health while delighting your taste. So, roll up your sleeves, gather your ingredients, and let the heart healthy Mediterranean Keto diet cookbook be your trusted companion on your health journey to a healthier, happier you. Bon appétit

Made in the USA
Las Vegas, NV
24 August 2024

94322057R00070